"How Do I Keep My Employees Motivated? is an imperative book for leaders in all fields. In order to motivate, you must be able to comprehend and connect on a personal level."

—TOM DASCHLE, former U.S. Senate Majority Leader

"George Langelett brings clarity to elements of management that we cherish at Markel. He explores the 'soft' topic of empathy-based management in ways that are highly accessible to managers who are compelled by 'hard' logic. He describes the scientific underpinnings of why empathetic management is successful, and he gives clear steps for how managers can develop such a style."

—ALAN I. KIRSHNER CHAIRMAN, CEO Markel Corporation

"I think this is an excellent book. Most books on motivation are either so heavy on theory and research that practicing managers may not know how to apply what's in the book or else rely so heavily on anecdotes and personal experiences to the point where validity suffers. This book, though, gets it just right: it is based on sound theory and research but offers truly usable applications and advice."

—DR. RICKY GRIFFIN, Department Head and Distinguished Professor of Management, Blocker Chair in Business, Mays Business School, Texas A&M University

"Individuals . . . [responsible for] guiding an intergenerational workforce in a nation of opportunity must have tools that network people together using positive methods of supervision. This book is a must read for every leader who desires to maintain motivated employees."

—SALLY DAMM, President & CEO, United Living Community

"Work has changed dramatically since relatively unskilled workers stood on production lines assembling widgets. Most work is highly skilled, complex, depends on teams, and requires judgment. In other words, it requires engaged employees at all levels. Management theory has evolved since the days of Scientific Management, but it has not always kept up. Dr. Langelett lays out the core goals of empathy-based management; establishes a practical and scientific foundation; and offers specific practices for work situations. To care about the work we do, it helps to care about the people with whom we work."

—BOB ROWE, President & CEO, NorthWestern Energy

"What an eye-opening approach to establishing staff motivation that doesn't need to start over with each new business cycle. Professor Langelett's explanation of the use of empathy as a motivational tool is the blueprint companies need to build and retain a quality staff in today's corporate America. The beauty of this concept is that it can be utilized staffwide as opposed to the traditional sales-only programs."

—GREG FARGEN, President, BankStar Financial Corporation

"I was pleasantly surprised by this book. I expected either a prescription for a new rewards program or an inspirational read with few useful strategies. Instead, the role of empathy presented in this book is clear, scientifically based, and fascinating to comprehend. I spent more time thinking about our management practices than reading. I wish this book had been available years ago; it presents a much more satisfying explanation of effective supervision than the platitudes I was taught in business school."

—LES HOWARD, Franchise Owner, Legacy Financial Partners

"I have shared [this book's] wisdom and life-transforming content with a number of my colleagues. What sets it apart from the rest is how Dr. Langelett weaves the critical aspects of empathy into leadership practices and guiding people behaviors. It also sets a new foundation and more humanistic approach to motivating employees and guided mindfulness in the workplace when it comes to building quality relationships that sustain quality organizations and cultures."

—ANNE BRUCE, author of *Discover True North, Manager's Guide to Motivating Employees*, and *How to Motivate Every Employee*

How Do I Keep
My Employees
Motivated?

THE PRACTICE OF

EMPATHY-BASED MANAGEMENT

GEORGE LANGELETT, PhD

RIVER GROVE
BOOKS

Published by River Grove Books
Austin, Texas
www.greenleafbookgroup.com

Distributed by River Grove Books

For ordering information or special discounts for bulk purchases, please contact River Grove Books at PO Box 91869, Austin, TX 78709, 512.891.6100.

Design and composition by Greenleaf Book Group LLC
Cover design by Greenleaf Book Group LLC
Cover image: © Getty Images (US), Inc. / Fuse

Publisher's Cataloging-In-Publication Data

Langelett, George.
   How do I keep my employees motivated? : the practice of empathy-based management / George Langelett, PhD.—First edition.
     pages ; cm
   Includes bibliographical references.
   ISBN: 978-1-938416-73-6
   1. Employee motivation. 2. Empathy. 3. Personnel management. 4. Interpersonal relations. I. Title.
HF5549.5.M63 L36 2014
658.3/14   2014933196

eBook ISBN: 978-1-938416-90-3

First Edition

CONTENTS

Dear Herbet,

Nice to meet You
at Aom

Please keep in touch,

Dedicated to Lara, Ian, and Ariana,
and to workers everywhere who
must endure unempathetic bosses.

PREFACE

In his *Wall Street Journal* article dated April 24, 2009, "How Business Schools Have Failed Business," Michael Jacobs asked several provocative questions in light of the 2008 collapse of the U.S. financial system. One of them was, "What have business schools failed to teach our business leaders and policy makers?" Jacobs pointed to corporate responsibilities and ethics, and he ended his article with this challenge: "America's business schools need to rethink what we are teaching—and not teaching—the next generation of leaders."[1]

Having taught management courses, including small business management and human resource management, at South Dakota State University for the past ten years, I had an unsettled feeling when I read Jacobs's article. I realized that I was very concerned about contemporary management textbook prescriptions for "how to" instill ethics into our business students and future leaders. The problem is a compatibility issue within the theory taught in today's college management courses, because motivation theory and behaviorism—or the use of rewards and punishments—is still widely taught. Offering people rewards inherently encourages the possibility of cheating and taking shortcuts in order to obtain the desired reward or outcome. This tendency contradicts my desire as an educator to instill ethical behavior within our future leaders.

Specifically, from my viewpoint as a college instructor, I have two fundamental concerns. First, the textbooks that I use in the classroom model employee decision making as a cognitive process in the employee's brain. This approach contradicts my understanding of how we humans make decisions. Both cognitive and emotional considerations factor into every decision we make. Without our emotions, we cannot make decisions. This reality may contradict orthodox contemporary management theory, but it is well understood in the field of neuroscience. Neurologist Antonio Damasio, in his book *Descartes' Error*, demonstrates that not only do emotions play a central role in our decision making, but our limbic region (the parts of our brain responsible for emotions) also regulates both our body's reactions and our brain's decision-making processes.

My second concern regards the assumed mechanism by which people become more ethical or unethical. The textbooks I use in class make suggestions, such as "Ethics starts at the top; employees will follow the manager's behavior"; and, "Make it a company practice to hire ethical employees." While these are excellent suggestions, they do not explain how a person becomes more ethical. Instead, they assume an employee is either ethical or unethical.

Contrary to practices in many companies today, a new hire does not become more ethical by reading the company handbook or by signing a statement of ethical behavior. Rather, for all of us, our behavior is determined by our desires and needs. If we view ethics as how we treat other people, the key to ethical behavior is an understanding of how our behavior affects the lives of others. Thus, empathy is the key to ethical behavior. The better a person understands how his or her actions affect other people, especially if they create hardship in others' lives, the more likely the person will behave ethically toward other people. By contrast, if a person does not recognize how his own behavior affects the well-being of others, his treatment of others becomes irrelevant. From my dissatisfaction with the textbook prescription for instilling ethics in our business students and future leaders, I started on a journey to better understand human nature, ethics, and what motivates people, particularly long-term motivation.

Teaching management courses at South Dakota State University has given me an opportunity to find answers. I started my search by digging into the contemporary management literature in order to better comprehend this widespread problem of the lack of understanding of how employees make decisions, and thus how managers can effectively build meaningful connections with each employee in order to improve satisfaction and performance. Unfortunately, contemporary management theory presented in academic management textbooks is deficient in its approach to employee motivation. Therefore my journey in writing this book has been a quest to present a comprehensive alternative approach to managing employee behavior, namely, an approach that is equipped to address both motivational and ethical issues. In order to better understand human behavior, I turned my attention from management literature to neuroscience literature.

After studying recent findings by neuroscientists, I was convinced more than ever that empathy is critical for both understanding and guiding employee behavior. My purpose in writing this book is to explain the importance of empathy in management practices and how managers can learn to apply empathy in order to alter the work environment in a positive manner for everyone involved.

As I began this journey, I realized that a natural starting point for this book was to reflect on a time in my own life when I was motivated to give my very best effort. Not because someone was dangling the proverbial carrot in front of my nose, but because I found an inspirational atmosphere that engaged my mind as well as my heart. That time period was my favorite year in school, the seventh grade. The reason is because of my science teacher that year, Mr. Norman, and the attributes he embodied and consistently demonstrated to his students. I didn't know to call it "empathy" back then, but that is in essence what characterized his relationships with middle schoolers. Empathy was the core of his behavior, which inspired me at a deeply personal level, and that is what I am striving to elaborate on in this book.

Each one of us—whether in the classroom or at work—desires to feel accepted and valued. We all are looking for someone who values us, enjoys working with us, and reciprocates our desire to form a close relationship. It is human nature to desire to find a mentor who unconditionally accepts us and with whom we enjoy working. When a mentor with whom we feel a personal connection is found, because we know that our mentor has our best interest in mind, we allow that person to help us through our problems and guide us along our journey in order to help us grow personally and to reach our potential. As our respect and esteem for that individual grow, we desire to please and work hard to perform at our highest ability. That secure bond becomes a source of purpose and motivation. Why and how does this occur? Further understanding of these issues is the focus of this book. I've written this book to present a new approach to motivation that will inspire the mind and earn the heart of each of your employees.

INTRODUCTION

If there is hope in the future, there is power in the present.
—ANONYMOUS

*While in the heat of emotion, it is a very poor
time to make any kind of decision.*
—JIM FAY

What motivates people to work hard at any task? As a manager, what can you do to motivate your employees to be fully engaged and give their best effort at their respective jobs? These are two eternal questions that the science of management seeks to answer. Today, much of the current philosophy of management regarding workplace motivation is focused on inducements or incentives. While well-thought-out incentives motivate employees in the short term, they lose effectiveness over time. In almost every case, as soon as an incentive program ends, employees change their behavior, and job performance slips. Worse yet, over time employees come to expect a new incentive program will be installed to replace the old program. And if a new incentive program is not initiated, employee morale will fall due to unmet expectations.

While employees will work hard for the correct incentive, often this approach feels detached and impersonal. Employees may actually feel manipulated or even "bribed" by management through incentive programs. Thus, although a reward or a punishment may capture the employee's attention and focus her effort as she responds according to the incentive, artificial inducements do not win the heart (loyalty) of each employee. Rather, employees are simply entering into an impersonal contract with management. So today, managers are realizing that traditional practices of rewards programs often feel mechanical, manipulative, and bureaucratic. Consequently, the programs often do not produce satisfactory results with regard to desired changes in employee behavior.

Gary Latham's book *Work Motivation* provides an in-depth review of the major theories of motivation developed during the twentieth century. During my reading, I was struck by two issues. First, the majority of the theories tended to focus solely on cognitive processes associated with human motivation. Recognition of human emotions and their effects on motivation was not a critical aspect of the influential management studies.

Second, I recognized something peculiar about business models of human motivation techniques: they were all man-made techniques. Each model tended to build on the work of previous published studies. Over time, this tendency drove the direction of the modeling of worker motivation behavior. Throughout much of the twentieth century, from Frederick Taylor to B. F. Skinner, prescriptions for motivating workers felt rather mechanical and emotionally detached.

I feel we have turned a corner and have started to better understand the nature of human motivation. Specifically, psychologists and managers have begun to model worker motivation as being influenced by both logic and emotions. Daniel Pink's influential book *Drive* suggests that once worker compensation is sufficient, employees are motivated by three issues: autonomy (vs. being constantly supervised), purpose (being able to see how one's work betters humanity), and mastery (the need to achieve professional excellence). All three are intrinsic or internal to each employee and are influenced by the neocortex (logical part) and the limbic (emotional) regions of our brains. After reading Pink's work, I am pleased that management literature is moving toward a better understanding of the nature of employee motivation.

Encouraged that managers understand that both logic and emotions influence the decisions that we make, I designed this book to help "push the envelope," or make further progress, in understanding how the human brain makes decisions, and how managers can both help employees make sound decisions and influence long-term motivation. I call this new approach empathy-based management. It is an alternative management approach that will allow you to connect with the hearts of each of your employees and create a work environment where they can be fully engaged, problem solve, and enjoy their work. This new approach is built on teaching you how to empathize, how to experience the emotions and comprehend the experiences of each of your employees.

If you look across professions outside of management, empathy is a key skill acquired for professional success. For example, years ago the counseling profession recognized that the key to helping each patient, despite the direst circumstances, was to give hope. Likewise, the marketing profession knows that salespeople who are able to empathize with customers are more likely to make a sale. During the recent wars in Iraq and Afghanistan, our military has been fighting against insurgents for the hearts and minds of the local populations. Our soldiers have learned that displaying empathy is the key to winning the hearts of the common people.

For you, a manager, the starting point for empathy-based management is the recognition that each person you employ is an individual with thoughts and feelings, dreams and fears, and a name. As you become more empathetic in dealing with each of your employees, their loyalty to and identification with you, their manager, and also the organization as a whole, are strengthened. Within an environment where an emotionally secure foundation is laid, each employee grows personally and professionally, to the benefit of both individual workers and the organization as a whole.

Reflecting on my own work life, I have had a number of bosses who were self-absorbed and poor communicators, and a few who were very arrogant in spite of being incompetent. Although I have no idea of their true motives, their words and actions created within me feelings of being neither respected nor valued. I felt as though they viewed me as an object or an expendable resource rather than a person with thoughts, feelings, and useful insights.

Unfortunately, I have listened to similar stories from people of all walks of life. But upon further reflection, I no longer blame individual managers for their lack of insight into what motivates people to be loyal and work hard. Rather, I believe this lack of understanding is a systemic problem within today's corporate America, driven by ever-increasing expectations for continual growth in profitability. Every three months Corporate America is under pressure to report earnings in line with analysts' expectations. Consequently, we have overlooked the fact that at the most basic level, every person employed in your organization desires two things: (1) to be understood and (2) to be accepted as a unique individual. Performance is a separate issue: we need to know that our level of productivity is acceptable. But at a much deeper or primal level, we need to be accepted for our humanity. Until workers feel unconditionally accepted for their own worth and human dignity, they will never be fully engaged in their work. They will work to comply, but they will put neither their hearts nor their loyalty into their jobs.

The underlying problem is that in order to be an effective supervisor and motivate employees, you, the manager, must matter to each worker. In order to matter, you must be able to relate to each employee on a personal level. If you do not matter, then you cannot help your employees reach their potential. If there is no emotional connection between a manager and an employee, the manager is irrelevant to the employee. An irrelevant manager cannot influence each employee's attitudes, behavior, level of motivation, or professional growth.

Some managers may be slightly uncomfortable with the idea of developing a "personal relationship" with each employee, and occasionally I am asked to define a personal relationship. Think of entering into a personal relationship as the opposite of a manager maintaining "professional distance" from each employee. Although there most likely will be no interactions with your employees outside of work, during the eight hours each day spent together at work, you enjoy the camaraderie of your employees. You may occasionally join your employees during lunch or a coffee break, share stories or a joke, and bring leftover dessert from last night's supper. Outside of work, you might attend an employee's wedding or a funeral of a family member. You may buy Girl Scout cookies from your employees' daughters, cut out newspaper clippings of their children winning Little League games, or organize a company office pool during March Madness. The actual activities you participate in are not important. What is important is that your employees identify with you as their boss and as a close friend who sincerely cares about their well-being.

In their book *Wired to Care*, Dev Patnaik and Peter Mortensen expand on this approach and suggest that management should care about the needs of all of the stakeholders in their organization. "It's just human nature to be interested in people who are interested in you . . . If you want to create products and services that other people care about, you should put aside your problems and start caring about other people's lives."[2] The underlying theory of empathy-based management is that *connection,* not *correction,* is required for professional development of your employees and management of employee behavior. People don't care how much you know until they know how much you care.

EMPATHY-BASED MANAGEMENT

The approach presented in this book is fundamentally different in both underlying assumptions and methodology from the traditional management practice of incentive programs. Traditionally, the focus of management has been on the company and, in particular, what is in the best interest of the organization. The underlying assumption of traditional management theory is that the purpose of employee motivation is to encourage or entice employees to work hard and maximize their productivity, which will benefit the company and have a positive impact on the organization's bottom line.

By contrast, the underlying assumption and starting point for empathy-based management is that the manager is working in the best interest of both the organization and the people employed by the organization. This means that the supervisor works hard to ensure that the employees grow professionally, become successful in life, and reach their potential. Competent, capable, ethical, and fully engaged employees will strengthen the performance of any organization. Helping each employee mature and become successful through professional development is one of the best investments any organization can make.

With empathy-based management, not only does the manager influence employees, but the employees also influence management. As the manager-employee relationship becomes stronger through trust and shared experiences, so does loyalty and identification with the organization. This felt connection, on a personal level, is a source of strength and an important employee asset that creates a foundation for the professional growth of both employees and managers. As one experiences professional growth, it often results in a desire to further excel professionally. Finally, the entire organization benefits from the professional growth occurring within everyone involved in this relationship.

AN OVERVIEW OF THIS BOOK

Keeping in mind the goal of empathy-based management is to create dedicated, ethical, competent, and enjoyable employees, this book will teach you the following four important concepts regarding empathy and its role in effectively managing employees.

1. Teach supervisors/managers a basic understanding of how the human brain functions and why empathy creates an environment in which employees can fully engage their brains in their work.

2. Explain how the ability to empathize with the emotional states and experiences of your employee is actually the driving force behind your employee desiring to develop a personal relationship with you. And that personal relationship is the foundation for developing a psychological bond with each employee, which becomes a source of emotional security and strength for each of your workers.

3. Teach you how to become a more empathetic manager and how to engage each employee on a personal level in order to create an emotionally secure environment where everyone can put their cognitive and emotional energy into their work rather than taxing their mental energy worrying about a variety of issues.

4. Explain how a personal relationship with another human being, especially one's supervisor, who is respected, creates a bond through which you can instill hope and which ultimately provides sustainable motivation. This book also explains why rules and temporary inducements fail to create sustainable motivation.

The immediate goal of empathy-based management is to create an emotionally safe and connected work environment. As a manager, you will learn how to calm down each employee's emotional state—including anger, fear, shame, and guilt—whenever the limbic region of the brain is triggered. This calming process will allow the employee to use the cognitive portion of her brain for thinking, problem solving, and decision making.

Also, for long-term cognitive growth and development, the human brain needs security and connection, not temporary inducements. Thus, employees grow professionally and are motivated to work hard for managers with whom they have developed a personal relationship. For each of your employees, an emotional connection to you, their supervisor, creates the psychological stability required for personal growth. As a manager, at first the prospect of building these connections might seem like a scary or even overwhelming skill to master. But over time, your ability to empathize effectively will become easier until it finally becomes intuitive. Much like mastering the skill of public speaking or learning to play the piano, your ability to read each person's emotional state and respond appropriately to your employee's concerns will soon become instinctual with practice. However, because every person and situation is unique, the ability to empathize and respond appropriately will always require you to concentrate and use a significant amount of emotional energy. In time your ability to empathize with each employee will feel natural and good and will benefit the personal growth of everyone involved in the experience.

ROAD MAP TO THIS BOOK

Each chapter in this book will address a specific issue in order to help you better understand empathy-based management and thus become a more empathetic manager.

Chapter 1 defines the term *empathy* and explains its importance in human relationships. I will look at the behavior of the human brain and demonstrate why empathetic relationships are critical for personal growth and the ability to reach one's potential. The final topic covered in chapter 1 is explaining empathy-based management.

Chapter 2 lays out the goals of empathy-based management: to create an emotionally secure work environment, to give each employee hope, and to help each employee grow personally and professionally. The ultimate goal of this chapter is to explore how empathy and personal connectedness create sustainable motivation when other methods fail.

In chapter 3 you will learn how to empathize when your employee is experiencing a crisis. You will learn about the concept of intersubjectivity, a fancy word for emotional experiences shared between two or more people. Through intersubjectivity you can join your employees in their experiences, both good and bad, with a sense of connectedness on an emotional level.

Chapter 4 lays out the tools you will need to empathize with your employees on a daily basis. The first half of the chapter is a guide to practices that are empathetic. The second half presents pitfalls to avoid. These pitfalls are included as guides to help you better understand the parameters of empathetic behavior.

Chapter 5 puts all of the different tools of empathy-based management into practice. This includes what to do, why it works, and how each technique calms down the limbic region, the emotional center of the human brain, and creates a sense of connection, hope, and feeling valued.

The book concludes with a summary of the highlights and key issues for practicing management based on empathy in any organization. Following the conclusion are appendixes and worksheets that are included to help you better understand the nature of empathy-based management and get you started in becoming more empathetic in your management practices.

· · ·

Management literature often treats empathy as a fixed personality trait. This assumption is incorrect. Much like learning how to drive a car, empathetic behavior is a skill that can be mastered with practice by virtually anyone.

1

EMPATHY: THE FOUNDATION FOR A NEW APPROACH TO MANAGEMENT

When we are understood, we feel affirmed and validated.
—STEPHEN COVEY

It is not our position, but our disposition,
that makes us happy.
—ANONYMOUS

Reflecting on both my childhood and my career, I can recall certain times when I have been very motivated to work hard. I noticed that during each period of peak motivation, I was under the tutelage of an authority figure I respected and admired. I have come to understand that the reason I felt a personal connection to specific authority figures—and not the numerous other potential authority figures—was because of each person's ability to empathize with my concerns.

You likely find that people who share your thoughts, feelings, and ideas are interesting. And you likely don't feel any connection with people who appear to have no interest in you. As with first impressions when dating, most of us can tell through the interactions following our first meeting with a new boss whether the relationship is going to be successful or disastrous. This sense is based on determining your boss's level of empathy—if she has the ability to walk in your shoes or if she doesn't seem to "get" you.

DEFINING EMPATHY

The dictionary defines *empathy* as "the intellectual identification with or vicarious experiencing of the feelings, thoughts, or attitudes of another."[3] This is the idea of walking in another person's shoes.

Although this explanation is clear, I prefer humanistic psychologist Carl Rogers's working definition of empathy: "Real communication occurs . . . when we listen with understanding. What does this mean? It means to see the expressed idea and attitude from the other person's point of view, to sense how it feels to him, to achieve his frame of reference in regard to the thing he is talking about."[4] I prefer Rogers's definition because real empathy becomes possible not by identifying with another person, but when we begin to have an understanding of what the person is experiencing and of the underlying problem, or why the person behaves a certain way. This understanding is the core of empathy, and it alone has the power to bind two people together.

Let's break down this understanding of empathy further. There are four steps to behaving with empathy. First, assume nothing. A good starting point is the honest recognition that you don't know the situation or the person's experience during the situation.

Second, listen with understanding. Give the other person your undivided attention; actively listen, and don't interject your own opinion into the matter. The key to listening with understanding is asking good questions. These questions include the following:

- "What just happened?"
- "Why did it occur?"

- "What was the chronological order?" i.e. What happened first, then what, etc.?
- "How is your employee interpreting the behavior of other people?"

These questions are aimed at providing meaning and clarifying your understanding of the other person's emotional experiences and what meanings the other person assigns to the event. You are trying to comprehend factually what happened, and also your employee's perception of the incident.

Third, refine your comprehension of what the other person is saying and experiencing. This may include asking additional questions for clarification, questions such as: So, may I summarize? Can I share with you what I believe you are saying, and please correct me if I have misinterpreted what you have just said. As you summarize, your employee will correct you by explaining the points that you do not fully comprehend. Often, step three is where actual understanding on your behalf occurs. When this understanding is realized, your employee can now experience your empathy with his or her predicament (perception of the event).

Fourth, respond in a way that honors the unique experience of the other person. (The goal of authentic empathy is always to help, never to harm a person experiencing a difficult situation.) By honoring, you give respect or show courteous regard that is appropriate for the situation. This appropriate response may include both words and actions. This fourth step is the key to being perceived as empathetic. Thus, it is important to remember that even though a person may possess great understanding of the experiences of another person, if the response does not honor the experience of the other person, the opportunity to display empathy will be lost.

Leadership coach Tanveer Naseer expands on Rogers's definition: "What empathy really means is being able to understand the needs of others. It means that you're aware of their feelings and how it impacts their perception. It doesn't mean you have to agree with how they see things; rather, being empathetic means that you're willing and able to appreciate what the other person is going through."[5] Thus, to empathize is to display understanding of another person's perspective, while withholding any and all judgment.

For example, if you have an employee who blames another employee for his work-related problems, to empathize means that you understand that from your employee's perception the other person is the cause of the problem. This does not mean that you agree with the employee.

Respected psychologist Arthur Ciaramicoli and coauthor Katherine Ketcham help to further explain the importance of empathy:

> By increasing our awareness of other people's thoughts and feelings, empathy shows us how to live life fully and wholeheartedly. Empathy is primarily interested in that process of becoming, enlarging, and expanding, for in truth that's what empathy is—an expansion of your life into the lives of others, the act of putting your ear to another person's soul and listening intently to its urgent whisperings. Who are you? What do you feel? What do you think? What means the most to you? These are the questions empathy seeks to explore. Playful and curious, always interested in the moment-to-moment interaction, empathy has the soul of a poet, the heart of a child, and the wisdom of a seer.[6]

Ciaramicoli and Ketcham consider empathy the expansion of your life into the lives of other people for the sake of understanding, alleviating loneliness, and instilling hope. Equally important, empathy creates camaraderie, companionship, and fellowship. It results in a perception of connection, importance, and an enjoyment of life.

ONE of the best examples of empathy comes from the book of Job in both the Jewish Tanakh and the Christian Bible. Job was a very wealthy man who, through three simultaneous tragedies, lost everything, including his family and his material wealth. We read:

"When Job's three friends . . . heard about all the troubles that had come upon him, they set out from their homes and met together by agreement to go and sympathize with him and comfort him. When they saw him from a distance, they could hardly recognize him; they began to weep aloud, and they tore their robes and sprinkled dust on their heads. Then they sat on the ground with him for seven days and seven nights. No one said a word to him, because they saw how great his suffering was."[7]

This is a wonderful example of how to empathize. Job's three friends did not try to cheer him up; rather, they behaved in a way that honored his emotional state. Job was suffering deeply, so his friends joined him in his pain and suffering. This is what it means to empathize. The manager does not deny the employee's feelings; rather, the manager joins the employee in his emotional state.

EMPATHY VS. SYMPATHY

Often, people confuse empathy with sympathy. The dictionary defines *sympathy* as the "fact or power of sharing the feelings of another, especially in sorrow or trouble; fellow feeling, compassion, or commiseration."[8] Embedded in this definition of sympathy is "commiseration," which has an element of feeling bad or sorry for the person.

The confusion between sympathy and empathy is unfortunate. The intention of sympathy is to commiserate with the person, in order to try and comfort. By contrast, the goal of empathy is to understand. To empathize is to not only understand the other person's emotional state or predicament from his or her perspective, but also to comprehend the underlying meaning and causes of one's feelings and behavior. This misunderstanding of the difference between sympathy and empathy is a serious problem because too often when we feel sorry for a person, we feel better, but the other person most likely will not feel better because no one with dignity wants other people to feel sorry for them. Even worse, an employee who is skilled in manipulation can use a manager's sympathy to his own advantage, including getting out of work or getting the manager to do things for him. By contrast, with empathy, you the manager are able to alleviate feelings of isolation, and with understanding real problem solving can occur.

UNFORTUNATELY, all too often people have dismissed the importance of empathy in the business world because they believe empathy is all about emotions rather than the use of logic. I have been told that empathy is too touchy-feely to be of any use in the real world. This lack of understanding is tragic for two reasons. First, the core of empathy is a logical understanding of what the other person is thinking and feeling. Second, if you are unwilling to learn how to empathize, you will be at a serious disadvantage competing against individuals who have mastered the skill of empathizing and are able to understand their employee's and customer's thoughts, feelings, desires, and perspectives. This ability to accurately understand the reasons behind another person's behavior is a very crucial skill to master in order to be successful in the business world.

WE ALL HAVE THE ABILITY TO EMPATHIZE

Occasionally, I have a student tell me that the idea of being able to empathize with another person's perspective sounds like a wonderful ability, but unfortunately, the student does not feel like she is very good at empathy. I respond with the fact that unless a person is a psychopath, each one of us has the innate ability to empathize.

Ciaramicoli and Ketcham explain that the ability to observe and interpret the nonverbal behavior of other people is already hardwired into our brains as an innate characteristic of human beings:

> We are constantly, if subconsciously, reading other people's emotions and thoughts by watching their facial expressions for subtle changes, noting the way they purse their lips, raise their eyebrows, or grit their teeth, observing the way their muscles shift to express tension, fear, or disgust, registering how they stand relaxed, hands in pockets, or nervously shift from one foot to the other. Through careful observation of other people's non-verbal behavior, we can infer, often with surprising accuracy, what they are thinking and feeling.[9]

As Ciaramicoli and Ketcham explain, for our own survival we have the ability to interpret the behavior of other people. However, for every human behavior and display of emotions, there are an infinite number of possible causes for a person's mood and disposition. Thus, even though observational empathy is a trait instinctually present within our nature, without practice, a person is unlikely to move beyond observing and interpreting behavior. By contrast, the goal of empathy-based management is not only to understand a person's behavior, but also to comprehend their perspective and the causes of the behavior.

NEUROSCIENCE SUPPORT

Now that you have a better understanding of what empathy is, it is important to consider what is happening inside the brain of each of your employees and how the human brain responds to your different behaviors. Physiological reasons determine why your employees respond in a particular way to your behavior. Fortunately, because of improvements in medical imaging over the past two decades, including functional magnetic resonance imaging (fMRI) technology, neuroscientists have made great advancements in both mapping and understanding the different portions of the human brain. Recent studies in neuroscience have begun to underscore the importance of empathy to the well-being and personal growth for each one of us. Also, neuroscientists, including Robert Sapolsky and Daniel Siegel, emphasize the importance of empathy in human interactions for the growth and development of the human brain.

As managers of employees, we need to update our theories to include empathy in regards to both employee behavior and how a manager motivates employees. Managers need to draw from this developing field of neuroscience and the importance of empathetic behavior when attempting to improve our ability to motivate employees.

I will divide this discussion of the workings of our brain into two parts, and summarize the major points pertinent to empathy at the end of this discussion. Part one focuses on the makeup of the human brain and how different regions of the brain respond to human relationships. You will see why perceived negative or strained relationships impair brain functioning, and by contrast, how empathy builds connections between human brains and is required for mental stability and growth. In part two, we will examine the parts of the human brain responsible for making empathy possible.

PART 1: STRUCTURE OF THE HUMAN BRAIN AND HOW RELATIONSHIPS MOTIVATE THE HUMAN MIND

Perhaps the simplest illustration of the human brain is Daniel Siegel's human hand model. Hold out your hand, tuck in your thumb, and wrap your four fingers over your thumb. You hand becomes a simple but very useful illustration of the human brain.

The wrist and palm of your hand represent the brain stem. The brain stem, also known as the "reptilian brain," controls the basic functions of the human body, including breathing, digestion, and regulating heartbeat. This is the part of the brain we share with reptiles. One could think of a reptile as a tube, with or without legs, and with teeth on one end. What do reptiles do? They eat, breathe, reproduce, and when in danger, they either fight or run away and hide. Beyond these basic instincts, not much thinking takes place. The entire function of the reptilian brain is self-preservation of its own existence.

The thumb tucked under your fingers represents the limbic region, also known as the "emotional center" of one's brain. This region includes the amygdala, the hypothalamus, cingulate gyrus, and hippocampi, one on each side, near your ears. At the core of the limbic region are the amygdala—two almond-shaped structures—that are an amazing part of the brain. Although other structures in the brain contribute to the formation of emotions, including the prefrontal neocortex, insula, and the cerebellum, the amygdala are the emotional alarm center of our brain and which signal different glands throughout our body to release hormones in response to our emotional state.

These functions of the amygdala are critical to human relationships. First, the amygdala are a social processing center. The amygdala assess every interaction we have with other people and animals, continuously monitoring every encounter for safety and danger. Emotional values are assigned to the behavior of other people during every social interaction, including: safe, dangerous, cold, warm, exciting, boring, pleasurable, painful, etc. The brain stores these emotional interpretations for future interactions with each individual. If a person has been assigned a negative feeling, such as dangerous, boring, strange, or creepy, the human brain will attempt to avoid interactions with the individual in the future. If the person is assigned a positive feeling, such as fun, interesting, safe, or exciting, the brain will seek to build on the relationship through future interactions.

Second, along with creating a wide variety of emotional states, the amygdala are also the brain's fight-or-flight alarm center. If at any time we consider another person's behavior unsafe, or if we see a person who in the past has been assessed to be unsafe, the amygdala will instantly cause the release of stress hormones that will immediately shift our entire body into fight-or-flight mode.

Within the limbic region, the hippocampus is attached to the amygdala. The hippocampus is responsible for determining what information is to be stored in the brain's long-term memory. The problem for the brain is that every day our five senses encounter millions of pieces of information to process. So, how does the hippocampus determine which pieces of information need to be stored into long-term memory? The hippocampus only stores events that have an emotional response associated with the encounter. The human brain is structured such that if the amygdala attach a strong emotional value to an event, then the hippocampus deems the event with the emotional attachment important enough to be stored in long-term memory. The other millions of pieces of information without any emotional importance are not transferred from working memory into long-term memory. For example, what do you remember from last year at this time? Most likely, you will not remember the exact details or itinerary of an average day. But if I ask you what you were doing on September 11, 2001, you most likely can remember the events of that day in great detail.

Two notes are worth mentioning regarding the hippocampus. First, it is one of the structures in the human brain most susceptible to chronic stress. Over time, exposure to high levels of chronic stress damages the hippocampus, and its ability to transfer important information into long-term memory becomes impaired. Thus, a highly stressed, poorly functioning hippocampus results in a reduction of information saved into a person's working memory. For example, if you recall a shared experience with a friend or coworker who has been under high stress for long periods of time, it is quite possible that she will have no recollection of the experience. Similarly, last-minute cramming for an exam stresses the hippocampus, and little pertinent information is committed to long-term memory. Plus, an exhausted brain has a horrible time trying to retrieve any information from memory.

Each employee needs a well-functioning hippocampus to do his or her job competently and effectively. For example, remembering a customer's name, troubleshooting unique problems, and remembering important details about each employee and important customers, including names of family members and birthdays, are all critical for success in a variety of jobs.

Second, the hippocampus is not mature until a child is around two-and-one-half years of age. If you think back to your childhood, your earliest memories likely start at around age two-and-one-half to three years of age. Without a mature, functioning hippocampus, we are unable to form explicit, long-term memories.

The third area of the brain, which is primarily responsible for complex cognitive processes, is the outside, called the cerebrum. These complex tasks include interacting and negotiating with other people, caring for our families, diagnosing and curing numerous diseases, harnessing nature to create a climate-controlled environment in which to live, diagnosing and solving a plethora of challenging problems in every field of study, and creating beautiful musical symphonies and aesthetically pleasing works of art. Like the canopy of a mushroom covering the stem, the cerebrum covers both the brain stem and limbic region. To understand the magnitude of the cerebrum, by one estimate, the brain stem contains around fifteen to twenty million nerve cells, and the limbic region contains around one hundred million nerve cells. Contrast this to the cerebrum, which is made up of one hundred billion nerve cells. The gray matter covering the brain is called the cerebral neocortex and is the area where our cognitive functions take place.

Specifically, the area in the front of our brain, called the prefrontal neocortex, is where reasoning and judgment take place. The region known as the dorsolateral prefrontal neocortex is where our actual mental processing takes place. Information from every area of our brain is sent to the dorsolateral prefrontal neocortex. After the dorsolateral prefrontal neocortex analyzes the information and makes a decision, the decision is relayed to the brain stem for the body to carry out, including the coordination of muscle movement in response to the decision.

One important fact managers should be aware of is that the prefrontal neocortex, responsible for sound judgment and decision making, does not mature until adulthood. Also, it matures faster in women than in men. This maturation of the prefrontal neocortex is the reason that car insurance rates are lower for female drivers than for males until they reach age twenty-five. Because of the immature prefrontal neocortex, good-natured, well-meaning young people will make errors in judgment. This lack of judgment will occur in every organization, and often, it will be more of a brain maturation issue than an issue of malicious intent. When this poor judgment occurs, a manager responding with empathy can mean the difference between an employee feeling humiliation and a teachable moment when personal growth and development can occur.

Perhaps surprisingly to some people, the limbic region controls the behavior of the human brain. As the human brain grows and matures, the limbic region and cortex become increasingly inter-twined. As these two regions merge, human reasoning and feel-ings increasingly influence each other. But whenever the brain is stressed or a person feels "under pressure," emotions will super-sede logic.

This role of the limbic region controlling the functions of our brain is described in detail by neurologist and neurobiologist Andrew Curran (2008):

> Emotions and our emotional brains underpin everything we learn, and the more you have connected with another human being emotionally the more they can learn from you[10] . . . What is also now known is that this wiring together of nerve cells is predomi-nantly under the control of your emotional system—the more emo-tion in a situation the more likely it is you will learn from it. So here is the second piece of understanding about brain functioning—the wiring together of nerve cells is predominantly under the control of your emotional system. This means that your emotional self is centrally involved in creating who you are.[11]

Now, the idea that emotions control our decision-making process may seem counterintuitive. After all, I firmly believe that I use logic, not emotions, whenever I make a decision. But the work of neurologist Antonio Damasio contradicts this notion. In his book *Descartes' Error*, Damasio demonstrates that not only do emotions play a central role in our decision making, but our limbic region regulates our decision-making processes. People with a damaged limbic region find themselves paralyzed by indecision. The reason is our limbic region uses the intensity of our emotions to calibrate our preferences. Without clearly established preferences, decision making becomes impossible.

More specifically, our amygdala is our alarm center for our brain. The amygdala respond much faster to threats than the neo-cortex of our brain. The amygdala respond with fight or flight in milliseconds, while the reaction time of the neocortex of our brain can be timed in seconds. Once the amygdala react, they immediately signals the hypothalamus, which controls our adrenal glands to release cortisol and epinephrine (adrenaline). The release of these stress hormones shuts down the cerebrum (neocortex) of our brain, shuts down our immune system, and elevates our heartbeat and our blood pressure. All thinking stops; we are ready to fight or run. Unfortunately, in many offices, this is a daily occurrence as the manager harshly reprimands employees. Each employee responds with anger and raised blood pressure and spends the rest of the day in fight-or-flight mode toward the manager, with no useful cognitive thinking taking place for the rest of the day. This is also why people who are under chronic stress are often physically sick. Raised levels of stress hormones over prolonged periods of time from chronic stress result in a compromised immune system.

This response in the limbic region is also the reason corporate incentive plans for employees often do not work as intended. The idea behind incentive plans is that if you place a reward in front of any employee, the person will work harder in order to earn the reward. Unfortunately, as Daniel Pink explains, a reward system has unintended effects on our brain.

> Like all extrinsic motivators, goals narrow our focus. That's one reason they can be effective; they concentrate the mind. But as we've seen, a narrowed focus exacts a cost. For complex or conceptual tasks, offering a reward can blinker the wide-ranging thinking necessary to come up with an innovative solution. Likewise, when an extrinsic goal is paramount—particularly a short-term, measurable one whose achievement delivers a big payoff—its presence can restrict our view of the broader dimensions of our behavior.[12]

Our amygdala sense the additional tension or stress caused by the potential reward, and our adrenal gland releases cortisol and epinephrine as our brain and body respond to the challenge at hand.

As planned by the manager, our cerebrum focuses on the source of this new tension, namely the potential reward, and guides our brain stem to do the required work, including muscle movements in order to achieve the reward. This is exactly the response that the manager wants from the employee. For jobs that require repetitive physical motion and no critical thinking, such as a cashier at a supermarket or a worker on an assembly line, reward systems work great for motivating employees.

The unintended problem is that when the stress hormones cortisol and epinephrine are released in our brain, our cerebrum focuses all of our cognitive energy on the source of the stress, namely achieving the reward, and this narrows the focus of overall thinking taking place in the brain. Therefore the unintended problem is that with a narrowed focus, by design of our cerebrum, we sacrifice our ability to think creatively and problem solve. One exception to this loss of creativity is that when a worker's cerebrum focuses solely on achieving a reward, she may use her cognitive abilities to achieve the reward through a creative method, including but not limited to, cheating in order to obtain the desired outcome.

Therefore any approach based on reward and punishment is no longer well suited for corporate America because over the past three decades most assembly-type jobs have been moved to developing countries. The majority of jobs that remain in the United States require problem-solving skills. For any job in your organization that requires either problem-solving skills or creativity, motivational programs based on rewards will create unintentional problems.

Ultimately, the reason that inducement-based approaches to employee motivation do not work well is because they are designed to control the behavior of people, keeping them subordinate to a manager's agenda. Reward systems are designed for compliance. They achieve compliance, but at an unintended cost; they create conformity and lower creativity.

For example, Teresa Amabile, a Harvard Business School Professor, conducted a study where a group of artists were each asked "to randomly select ten commissioned works and ten noncommissioned works" to be judged. The "commissioned works were rated as significantly less creative than the noncommissioned works, yet they were not rated as different in technical quality."[13] The artists' comments suggested that commissioned works were more stressful to paint because of higher internalized expectations from being paid. The stress felt by the artists' amygdalas resulted in less creative works of art.

Thus, rewards and punishments tend to focus the human brain on the pending incentive and reduce our creative ability that we could apply to the task at hand if our brain did not feel stressed. Even worse things occur in the human brain when a manager tries to control employee behavior through shaming the worker. Shame results when a manager attacks the person rather than confronting the behavior. When experiencing a deeply shaming reprimand, the amygdala interprets the experience as beyond fight or flight; the attack is treated as a personal attack on the psyche. It has the potential to do permanent damage to a person's sense of well-being. Feeling the impact of being shamed, the amygdala signals to the brain stem that the situation is critical for self-preservation, and the brain stem shuts down both the neocortex and limbic region. As part of the limbic region, the amygdala get shut down. Similar to a turtle retracting into its protective shell, the person becomes physically paralyzed and only the brain stem is operational.

Anyone who has experienced being shamed knows that it is a horrible sensation. When I have felt shamed, I just wanted to find someplace to hide or disappear to, where no one can see me. When shamed, a person cannot think, they have no feeling—only an overwhelming sense of becoming numb, or they have the urge to vomit as a result of the shame. The sensation of being nauseous results from our brain stem being the only part of our brain that is still functioning unimpaired.

By contrast, if an employee of an empathetic manager does something wrong and knows he will be required to face the consequences of his actions, he will still feel safe. The employee also senses an authentic connection as his manager comprehends his experience. In spite of the mistake, the manager respects the employee as a person and desires that the employee experience a teachable moment in order to learn from the mistake, with the end goal to give the person the opportunity to grow from the experience. In other words, the employee knows that the manager has his best interest in mind. As a result, the employee feels connected to his boss, and his hypothalamus signals the pituitary gland to release oxytocin, the bonding hormone. The release of oxytocin calms the amygdala, and the entire limbic region feels safe and secure. The calm and stable limbic region gives the employee the opportunity to use the neocortex of his brain to rationally learn from a mistake. After sensing his boss's understanding and experiencing a sense of connectedness, the employee is freed to use his brain to its full potential for creative problem solving and innovative thinking.

But there is also a long-term benefit to working for an empathetic manager. Remember that, like the cap of a mushroom, the front of the brain wraps around the prefrontal cortex, which is physically next to the amygdala. Within a stable environment, under the tutelage of an empathetic supervisor, as the brain develops over time, the prefrontal cortex can grow connections or synapses with the cells of the amygdala. Once these connections are built, the prefrontal cortex can help regulate the amygdala, and the employee can then use logic and reason to calm down his limbic region. Emotional self-regulation becomes possible in a safe environment, but it is impossible for this physiological development to occur in the human brain of someone who performs work in an emotionally unsafe or stressed environment.

Therefore, within the context of neuroscience, the reason to practice empathy-based management is to create a stable environment where the brain of each employee can continue to grow and develop in order to learn new tasks and jobs and master each. Over the past two decades, neuroscientists discovered that humans do not have a static or fixed level of intelligence. Rather, each of our brains has the ability to rewire itself and create new connections so that we can learn new tasks and, with focus and repetition, can master nearly any task. Researchers call this phenomenon the neuroplasticity of the human brain. For example, almost anyone with practice and dedication can learn to ride a bike, type on a computer, work algebra problems, or understand a foreign language. Learning each of these skills may take a lot of hard work, but with encouragement and dedication, anything becomes possible for our brains. Professor Mark Hickson III and Dr. Christie Beck (2008) underscore the importance of environment on the development of our brain:

> An important point about the evolution of the brain is that the synapse of every neuron is not genetically predetermined. There are not even enough genes to determine the exact structure and order of every synapse in the brain. The genome sets a general arrangement of systems and circuits in the modern brain sectors, but the precise arrangement is under the influence of the environment.[14]

Because our brains are not genetically preset, the environment in which each person lives will determine the connections created between their brain cells. There is a saying in neuroscience that "nerve cells that fire together, wire together."[15] But over time, one's environment and repetition of behaviors determines which cells fire together. This is why a supportive work environment is imperative for each employee's optimal brain growth and development over time.

PART 2: PARTS OF THE HUMAN BRAIN RESPONSIBLE FOR MAKING EMPATHY POSSIBLE

The human brain's ability to detect, understand, and feel what emotions other people are experiencing is an amazing feat. Neuroscientists are now beginning to understand how our brain is able to accomplish these tasks. In this section we will briefly examine four brain structures that make empathy possible. Keep in mind that all of these discoveries have occurred very recently, and there is still much work to be done regarding how our brains are able to empathize with other brains.

To start, no one structure in your brain is responsible for your ability to empathize. Rather, regions of your brain work together in order to make empathy possible. This is similar to how no one part in a car's motor is responsible for creating power. The carburetor, spark plug, piston, and crankshaft all work together to turn air and gasoline into mechanical power.

In 2005, neuroscientists made the amazing discovery that the same neurons light up whether we are performing a task or watching the task being performed by someone else. These neurons, located in the frontal and parietal lobes of the brain cortex, were named "mirror neurons" because they respond and learn the same by watching the experiences of other people. Numerous examples exist of the results of these mirror neurons. Sports fans can become very emotional watching their favorite team play. Fans celebrate with excitement with the team's victory, and become sad or angry when their favorite team loses an important game. The mirror neurons allow us to "experience" the intense emotions others experience.

Scientists are discovering that our anterior temporal lobes, on the sides of our brain, perceive and model the social behavior of other people. This region stores and retrieves information on social behavior learned from other people. This is a part of what neuroscientists call semantic memory, memory that can be implicit or subconscious. Thus, it is possible to copy the behavior of another person and not even be aware that we are displaying the same conduct and mannerisms as the other person. This is one reason why parents become concerned about the influences of peer pressure on their teenage children. But people of all ages learn by mimicking the behavior of other people, especially individuals whom we trust and respect.

A third structure in our brains that is important for empathy also lies within our temporal lobe. The superior temporal sulcus region perceives where other people are gazing (the focal point of their eyes). From determining the other person's focal point, this region of the brain interprets where the other person's emotions are directed. Hearing another person's voice also activates this area of the brain.

The cingulate cortex, a structure in the limbic region of your brain, is the fourth and final structure that is very important for human empathy. The cingulate cortex is the regulator of our brain and body. This portion of the limbic region is connected to all three parts of the brain: the brain stem, limbic region, and neocortex. It continuously monitors our body's physiological processes, including respiration and blood pressure, and also our emotions, for any errors or problems. When our cingulate cortex is functioning properly, we can regulate our own emotions, and with stable emotions, empathy for other people's emotions occurs through our mirror neurons. But when a person's cingulate cortex is damaged or functioning poorly, the ability to regulate one's own emotions becomes very difficult or impossible. It must function properly for our brains to empathize with the emotional experiences of other people. For a person experiencing difficulty in controlling his own emotions, this inability to self-regulate becomes a barrier to empathizing or experiencing the emotions of another person.

NEUROSCIENCE AND ETHICS

As a result of the recent work in neuroscience, researchers and managers are beginning to understand that ethical behavior in the workplace today does not result from reading an employee handbook. Rather, ethical behavior results from our brain's ability to empathize with other people. Particularly important is our ability to see beyond ourselves and our actions. Once we can empathize and experience how our self-focused behavior has negative consequences on the well-being of other people, we will likely change our behavior.

Unfortunately, as Patnaik points out, the behavior of most corporations today is incongruent with the findings from neuroscience regarding human behavior:

> By this standard, most companies are corporate iguanas. It's as if they've skipped right over the limbic region to grow a neocortex . . . Without a limbic system, companies lack any sense of empathy or courage. They're either all neocortex, analyzing thoughtfully without the motivation to act, or reptilian, caught in a cycle of fight-or-flight responses. That's deeply unfortunate, because companies are made up of people, not iguanas. And people, not iguanas, buy products and services.[16]

It is my sincere desire that, as more managers understand the importance of empathy, the culture of corporate America will change. As more executives practice empathetic behavior, they experience the impact of unethical behavior on other persons, and it leads to real change within the culture, rather than corporations relying on company policies to guide ethical behavior.

FROM neuroscience we learn that the importance of empathy-based management is threefold: (1) to prevent the brain from releasing stress hormones, including cortisol, and thus shutting down each employee's ability to think and problem solve; (2) to encourage the release of oxytocin, which calms the amygdala in our brain so each employee can focus on the task at hand, rather than being preoccupied and focused on one's emotions; and (3) to reduce stress on the hippocampus, so that it functions properly and employees can remember the important information that is required to problem solve and be effective at their jobs.

WHAT IS EMPATHY-BASED MANAGEMENT?

Through neuroscience, we are now able to understand that a sense of connection and environmental stability are required for our brains to grow and reach their potential. Particularly important in the development of each employee's brain is the behavior of the worker's immediate supervisor, as well as management practices throughout the organization. With the focus on the behavior of the human brain, the need arises for empathetic behavior on behalf of management.

I define empathy-based management as a new protocol in which a manager's ability to empathize is a prerequisite to effectively performing the duties of management, including planning, organizing, leading, and controlling.

This managerial protocol is built on the manager's practice of understanding and honoring the thoughts, perceptions, ideas, experiences, concerns, and reactions of all stakeholders in their organization, including customers, employees, suppliers, and investors.

As mentioned in the introduction, every person in your organization has the need to be understood and accepted. When your employee feels understood and accepted, he feels safe and comfortable. He feels he fits into your organization. When an employee doesn't feel understood or accepted, he'll likely leave to find a new organization where he will feel more welcome. With this reality, it is imperative that as a manager you understand the experiences and concerns brought to your attention by each employee. With empathy-based management you can learn the process of how to understand your employees' concerns and respond in a manner that honors each employee's unique problems. In the process of honoring the concerns of each employee, you create an emotionally safe work environment within your organization.

Naseer helps explain the role of empathy in management:

> You gain a greater awareness of the needs of your employees. Empathy allows you to create an environment of open communication and more effective feedback. It allows us to understand and explore problems employees face and how to help them resolve them. Being empathetic with your employees helps to validate what they're going through.[17]

From the manager's ability to effectively communicate understanding comes the ability to validate each person's experiences. Through validating each person's perspective, empathy-based management creates an emotionally secure organization in which all stakeholders can use their cognitive and creative energies to problem solve and contribute to the success and well-being of their own careers and the organization as a whole. In the absence of an emotionally secure work environment, employees waste enormous amounts of emotional energy dwelling on problems and concerns that they believe may never get resolved or even addressed.

Within an emotionally secure work environment where workers have certain, steady, and secure relationships with their supervisor, personal relationships are not threatened by miscommunication, consequences, or different points of view. An employee in this type of work environment knows that no matter what she does, she will be required to face the consequences of her actions. But she also knows that her relationship with her manager will be repaired and remain intact. An emotionally secure work environment becomes the foundation of worker morale in any organization.

The employee recognizes that the manager can direct and guide her, and she can discuss issues, disagree, argue, and even get angry with her manager with complete confidence that her personal relationship with the manager will remain intact. Her relationship with her manager is secure and will remain warm and meaningful despite any disagreement. She has complete confidence that an intense disagreement, miscommunication, or misunderstanding may cause a temporary psychological break in the relationship, but the break is always temporary. Temporary breaks in the relationship are followed by a deliberate effort by the manager to repair any damage and restart the relationship.

An emotionally safe work environment provides each employee with the opportunity to have a calm and stable limbic region. With a calm affective portion of the brain, the employee can make full use of the cognitive portion of the brain in order to learn new skills, problem solve, and grow personally and professionally.

CONCLUSION

In summary, empathy can be defined as real communication that occurs when we listen with understanding and respond in a way that honors the unique experience of others. From neuroscience, we saw the importance of empathy in calming the limbic region in our brain so that we can use our cerebrum for critical thinking and problem solving. At its core, empathy-based management is simply a management style in which you understand and honor the concerns of each of your stakeholders.

Chapter 2 examines the core goals of empathy-based management. As you will read, the end goals are to create more satisfied customers and employees, more competent and productive employees, and ultimately increased profitability and growth for your department and the organization as a whole.

2

CORE GOALS OF EMPATHY-BASED MANAGEMENT

Empathic listening is always centered on the other person,
and its goal is to make the other feel uniquely understood.
—ARTHUR CIARAMICOLI

If the manager doesn't care, the employees don't care.
—ANONYMOUS

In a competitive global economy, your organization may face new challenges each day. The challenges for every organization will come from a wide variety of internal and external sources. Some challenges will be foreseeable; others will not. In order for your organization to survive and prosper no matter the business climate, your company will need to respond creatively, resourcefully, and effectively to each new problem that arises. With empathy-based management your organization will be able to grow and thrive in any business climate. To do so requires that your organization comprehend the nature of the problem and have a workforce capable of overcoming each problem through using critical thinking and problem-solving skills.

As Patnaik explains, empathy not only allows your organization to understand the nature of external problems, it also allows your company to recognize opportunities before your competitors do.

When people in an organization have an implicit understanding of the world around them, they make a thousand better decisions every day. They're able to see new opportunities faster than companies that rely on secondhand information . . . Empathy drives growth because it tells an organization what's valuable to the people outside its walls . . . Sometimes having an empathic connection to the world around you can reveal huge opportunities that everyone else was missing. Sometimes it can reframe how you see the world.[18]

Patnaik was referring to gaining a competitive advantage by the ability to see what no one else has noticed. As the global business environment is constantly changing, through the use of empathy, not only can you stay one step ahead of your competition through understanding the opportunities and threats that come with change, but more importantly, empathy can be used to create the internal readiness and nimbleness required for your organization to be able to effectively adapt and take advantage of each opportunity.

Along with your ability to understand other people's perspectives, for long-term success you must also understand employee behavior. For your organization to continuously solve each new problem that arises, you will need a workforce that is motivated and competent at their respective jobs. But competence alone will not suffice. You will also need employees who are motivated to problem solve and create innovative solutions to each new problem as your organization experiences change. Although there are numerous applications for empathy-based management, this book is focused on providing you with the ability to develop employees who are motivated to work competently at their jobs and to problem solve and create innovative solutions to any challenge that your company should face.

THREE INTERMEDIATE GOALS THAT LEAD TO YOUR END GOAL

Here, your end goal is to develop employees who stay motivated, work competently, and problem solve throughout their professional careers. You now need to fill in the necessary steps along the way in order to reach your goal. In this chapter we will examine the three intermediate goals required to make the end goal possible: (1) to create an emotionally secure work environment; (2) to give each employee hope; and (3) to help each employee grow personally and professionally. You will see that each of these goals supports and enriches the others in a reinforcing cycle and that your entire organization benefits as each employee matures in this manner.

Goal #1: Create an Emotionally Secure Work Environment

The first goal of empathy-based management is to create an emotionally secure work environment on a daily basis for all employees. This will help to calm down each employee's limbic region, particularly the amygdala, during periods of high stress and times of crisis.

According to Marcia Moran of Positive Business DC, empathy on behalf of leadership is critical during times of crisis: "To respond appropriately to crises, the person at the helm of an organization also needs to exhibit emotional empathy. Our brains are wired to respond to the emotions of others on a very personal level. Connecting emotionally draws people in and creates trust." [19]

For example, if one of your company's largest and most important customers cancels their order and makes it clear that they will no longer be a customer, a manager could respond in one of two manners. The manager could display extreme stress from the lost account, telling the sales force and workforce that "our company is in financial trouble and everyone needs to work twice as hard and think creatively in order to find new customers and recover the lost sales." In this case, the employees would empathize with the manager's display of stress and become distressed themselves. They may become irritable and feel that the manager's behavior is "unfair" since they have done nothing wrong. A stressed, unenjoyable work environment would result.

Or the manager could display more empathetic behavior, telling the employees that the company's largest account has been lost but the company will be OK because the employees are competent and have great ingenuity for problem solving. Therefore, as a company, they will be able to figure out how to handle the problem. Though the customer canceling the account is a setback, the manager must convey that the company is able to handle it. In this case, the manager's calm response reassures the employees and prevents them from becoming stressed and triggering the brain's amygdala. With a calm limbic region, they can focus on their work and think about creative solutions to this problem. The employees' connection to a calm, empathetic leader is a source of strength and reassurance during this difficult period of time.

On a daily basis, within an emotionally secure environment, every person in the organization experiences being understood and appreciated by the leadership of the institution. Everyone has the freedom to express her own individual interests, beliefs, and ideas, and the manager takes the time to comprehend what is being said and responds with understanding and appreciation. Provided an emotionally safe environment, each employee has the opportunity to work under conditions that deliberately calm down the amygdala in order to stabilize the limbic region of each person's brain. With a calmed limbic region, the employee can make full use of the cognitive portion of her brain in order to problem solve and grow personally and professionally (goal three).

Every job in an organization involves stress. *Merriam-Webster's* defines *stress* as "a constraining force or influence: such as a physical, chemical, or emotional factor that causes bodily or mental tension and may be a factor in disease causation."[20] Stress in the workplace comes from multiple sources, including (1) forces external to the organization, including competition, uncertainty, and the economy; (2) internal forces, including the structure and management style of the organization; and (3) the job itself, including requirements to concentrate and problem solve, deadlines, and physical movements. One of the purposes of empathy-based management is to minimize stress resulting from forces within the company. This is achieved through management understanding and supporting each employee; clear, multidirectional communicating from open access and teamwork with management; and employees at all levels of the organization behaving ethically, treating each other with respect, respecting other people's property, and supporting one another.

Even though stress within the organization is minimized, there will always be stress from both outside competitive forces and from the job itself. Because it is impossible, and not necessarily desirable, to remove all stress from the workplace, there will always be a need for empathetic managers who can help each employee effectively deal with stress and problems, embody understanding, and ultimately impart hope.

Ultimately, the reason to create an emotionally secure work environment is so your employees can undividedly focus their cognitive and creative abilities on the tasks at hand in order to move your company forward.

Jack Welch, former CEO of General Electric, summarized this idea very concisely: "I think any company . . . has got to find a way to engage the mind of every single employee . . . If you're not thinking all the time about making every person more valuable, you don't have a chance. What's the alternative? Wasted minds? Uninvolved people? A labor force that's angry or bored? That doesn't make sense."[21]

Goal #2: Give Hope

How does an approach based on empathy keep people motivated over the long term? The crucial factor required for a person to be motivated is *hope*. Hope—which stems from the employee trusting and being understood by an empathetic manager—is the elixir of sustainable motivation. It is simply the belief that one's life and circumstances will either get better or continue to improve. Without hope, sustainable motivation is not possible. This reality was best summed up by leadership expert John Baldoni: "With hope, individuals can see over the edge of adversity; they can look beyond where they stand now . . . Without hope, nothing is possible. With hope, everything is possible."[22]

Hope and empathy are intimately related. Empathy is two people joining together in a common understanding. It is required if a manager is to instill hope in an employee. The manager builds a personal relationship with the employee through empathy. Thus both trust and understanding are the prerequisites for the manager's goal of offering the employee hope. Without these two legs to stand on, hope is not possible.

TRUST AND EMPATHY IMPART HOPE

PREREQUISITE #1 TRUST

The key emotion that underlies any relationship of value is trust. Only after trust has been established can a person influence the emotions of another person, both positive and negative. Douglas McGregor, the father of Theory X and Theory Y (see Appendix A), defined trust as the "knowledge that you will not deliberately or accidentally, consciously or unconsciously, take unfair advantage of me. I can put my situation at the moment, my status and self-esteem in this group, our relationship, my job, my career, even my life, in your hands with complete confidence."[23]

A manager must earn the employee's trust. Otherwise, any attempt to change the employee's mood will only conjure negative emotions because the person will feel manipulated. The attempt will feel phony, or part of an agenda, and will not be taken seriously. To be considered trustworthy, the person must be perceived as authentic in both personality and agenda. To be authentic means one has integrity, or a person who keeps one's word. A person with integrity is the same on the outside as on the inside, and her nonverbal behavior matches her words. The manager must demonstrate through both words and actions that her intention to keep the employee's best interest as her priority is genuine.

PREREQUISITE #2 EMPATHY

Clinical psychologist and professor at Columbia University, Xavier Amador, explains the importance of the ability to empathize when you are trying to manage another person's behavior this way: "Whenever you want to facilitate change in another person, you must first become his friend (i.e., someone he trusts). Whenever you convey empathy for another person's experience, he feels understood, respected, and more trusting. Because you understand the other person's point of view and how he feels about his situation, there is nothing to argue about. Consequently, he becomes less defensive and more open to hearing your perspective."[24]

Empathy also results in an emotional bond between two people. This emotional bond becomes a source of strength for both individuals. When your employee feels safe and secure, he no longer is required to expend emotional energy being on guard for possible threats. Instead, he can devote his energy and talent to the task at hand. Over time, the secure emotional bond with one's supervisor creates a safe foundation from which an employee can relax and be her true self, take risks, utilize creativity, learn, and grow.

Although within the field of management hope has been often overlooked as the key to long-term motivation, other fields recognize the importance of hope in motivating people. Within the counseling profession, when working with any patient, what is the one key thing that any counselor can do in order to help her patient improve? The answer: provide hope. Likewise in the field of marketing, why is each "motivational speaker" actually considered to be motivational? Answer: the speaker gives the listener hope—that is, hope to make money, enjoy better health, solve a problem, create a better future, etc. Do the lives of people actually turn out as promised by the speaker? In many cases, the answer is no. But this answer is irrelevant. As long as the speaker can create a feeling of hope within people, people will buy whatever product the speaker is selling because the feeling of hope motivates people into action.

Goal #3: Help People Grow Personally and Professionally

The third goal of empathy-based management is helping each of your employees grow personally and professionally. This is accomplished through three basic steps: listening to, removing barriers for, and investing in each employee. Let's look at each of these steps in detail. (Note: In chapter 4 I'll explain each step in more detail when I outline the tools managers can use to learn how to empathize.)

Step 1: Listen: Give Your Undivided Attention

Within my own career in academia, I have worked for more than a dozen deans and department heads. Like most employees, within thirty seconds of starting a conversation with each supervisor, I can tell if the person is interested in what I have to say or is so preoccupied with his/her own agenda that what I say is not important to the person. As soon as I sense that the other person would rather not listen to me, I simply tell my supervisor, "Oh, I am sorry; I can see that you are very busy right now. We can visit when you are not so busy." The supervisor often replies either "I am sorry" or "Oh, thank you." And often, unfortunately, this is the end of our conversation. If the behavior is repeated, it is the end of a trusting relationship with my superior.

The first step requires you, the manager, to actively listen to your employees. Active listening requires your undivided attention. Being aware of your body language throughout the entire conversation is critical. Is your body language conveying that you are relaxed, open, and interested in what the employee has to say? Or are you preoccupied with something during the conversation? Also, are you listening to the employee's words for understanding? Or are you thinking ahead of how to word your response? Active listening requires you to listen for comprehension, and this cannot be accomplished if you are preoccupied with your own thoughts.

Once your employee is finished speaking, pause in order to allow your brain to fully comprehend what your employee just told you, and then take time to formulate your response, or ask a question for further clarification. In any conversation it is OK to delay your response a few seconds. A delay signals that you are taking the other person's comments seriously and are taking the time to formulate an appropriate response.

Through active listening, you will learn who the employee is as a person, his interests and needs, and the barriers in his life that prevent him from being successful. Using the vocabulary of noted psychologist Abraham Maslow in his theory of human motivation, your intention is to help the individual reach self-actualization—the highest of the five tiers of the hierarchy of human needs.

Finally, it is a good idea, after visiting with your employee, to take notes about key issues, names, and events that you talked about, while the conversation is still fresh in your mind. Then, before future conversations with each employee, review the notes from past conversations. This will help to strengthen your understanding of each employee as a unique individual as you learn to become a more empathetic manager.

Step 2: Remove Barriers

The second step involves the manager working to remove as many barriers as possible that society puts in front of each employee. These barriers cause people to become stuck and display reduced energy and motivation because they cannot move forward with their lives. Thus, by removing barriers in their work lives, a manager gives people energy or drive (or life). The human spirit can be an amazing force to encounter once people are released from the barriers holding them back.

One such barrier takes the form of labels with which an individual or his status is described and often internally defined. Labels stick, and it is hard for a person to remove a label once she is labeled by society. Labels are also meant to control people and to dehumanize them, turning a person into an object. The manager's job is to remove these labels.

For example, often people are labeled based on their beliefs or worldview. These labels seem to be benign. Examples include liberal or conservative; Democrat, Republican, or Libertarian; Christian, Jew, Muslim, Hindu, Buddhist, agnostic, or atheist; etc. The problem with these seemingly benign labels is that they create stigmas and a mentality of "us versus them." Within your department, you cannot afford this mentality. Every person in your company is a crucial member of your team. If someone on your team insists on building an "us versus them" mentality, target your company's *competitors* as the "them." In order for your company to compete today, you need the utmost effort from every one of your employees. As I point out repeatedly throughout this book, the reality is that we are all human, with a need to be accepted, understood, and valued in order to engage both our hearts and minds.

Another type of labeling seen in workplaces relates to a person's academic background. For example, if someone does not have a high school diploma, society calls that individual "a high school dropout," which has a strong negative connotation. More importantly, the stigma associated with not completing high school limits the person's ability to advance in many organizations. If an employee does not have a high school diploma, the empathetic manager helps the employee secure the necessary resource—such as child care, tuition reimbursement, transportation, and a compatible work schedule—so he can earn his GED.

Likewise, many organizations today require a college diploma for an employee to advance into management. If an employee does not have a college degree, the manager can motivate the employee by encouraging and helping her to earn an associate's degree or a bachelor's degree. With a college degree in hand, many new opportunities will become available to your employee. These new opportunities will help your employee reach her potential. No matter which path your employee chooses to reach her goals, she will always retain a lifelong connection to you and your organization for helping her get her degree.

As you get to know each employee on a personal level, it may become apparent that certain employees may have personal problems that have become serious barriers to their well-being. These problems may be external, including living in an abusive family or having an abusive spouse/partner. Or the problems may be internal, from a wide variety of harmful behaviors, including drug and alcohol addiction. An empathetic manager will acknowledge the underlying hurt and pain, sorrow, and depression, and encourage workers to avail themselves of an employee assistance program to deal with issues of addiction, spousal abuse, etc. Or, if your company doesn't offer such treatment options in the employee benefits package, the manager will become a champion for adding this important resource to what the company provides. Once the addiction or abuse can then be effectively treated, the employee is given her life back. How you actually acknowledge your employee's deep underlying pain and despair will be explained in chapters 3 and 4.

Step 3: Invest

The third step is for the manager to invest in each employee. Recalling our discussion of the human brain in chapter 1, the empathetic manager creates an emotionally safe work environment in which each employee experiences stability and connectedness that is conducive for personal and professional growth. Beyond this basic investment, an empathetic manager is proactive in seeking professional development opportunities for each employee.

As you get to know them on a personal level and discover their talents and interests, give each employee assignments that will help them grow in their area of interest. This may include both formal and informal training for the employee. Make sure to give each employee both the authority and needed resources to be successful at each new assignment.

Beyond on-the-job training programs, encourage your employees to attend external programs that will be useful for their professional development. Have your employees attend trade association meetings, take evening classes—both for credit and noncredit—and complete certificate programs. Encourage them to attend seminars from nationally known experts speaking in your area. Provide opportunities for each employee to travel, and expand both their view of the world and their comfort zones.

Perhaps the single most important thing you can do is to listen to each employee. Each employee is a unique person with unique dreams and goals. Listen to your employees and create an ongoing dialogue as to what can be done in order to facilitate their ability to reach their professional goals and dreams. Along the way, suggest professional development opportunities as they arise.

Also, as you spend time with each person on a daily basis, it will become obvious that particular employees have issues underneath the surface that are impeding their growth and development. Often this is a result of either a neglectful or abused past. With no one previously investing in this person, the employee has few internal resources to contribute to your organization. For example, some of your employees will have the required technical competencies, but they might lack social skills to be fully accepted by their peers. Other employees may be very intelligent but lack impulse control, and this lack of self-control is a source of continual problems in their lives.

As a manager, you have the opportunity to invest in these employees. This includes developing a personal relationship with each one and being a rock of stability in their lives. One of the powers of empathy is to understand another person's emotional state and to have the ability to calm the person down through communicated understanding and unconditional acceptance. In most cases, a consistently firm but gentle and reassuring presence is required to point the person in the right direction and keep them on the path as they proverbially take two steps forward and one step backward.

At first, progress may be slow or negligible, but once trust has been established, hope becomes possible. With hope, personal growth may begin. Each time your employee slips back into self-defeating behaviors, you have an opportunity to calm him down so he can think clearly about his behavior and the resulting consequences, and make better choices. As your consistently empathetic presence calms his emotions, an opportunity arises to discuss dreams and ideas and have a conversation about how to create a path for him to realize his dreams.

As you invest in each of your employees, your labor force will then have more talent and internal resources to contribute to the company. This investment results in greater employee loyalty. But in order for loyalty to be created, the investment needs to be sincere, authentic investment, and not a temporary inducement.

Finally, and in my opinion most importantly, develop an investment mindset such that your investment goal is to have each employee outgrow your company with their professional development. Although this may sound self-defeating, this is actually the best mindset toward employee investment. It is true that some employees will leave your organization for better opportunities. But, unfortunately, millions of workers today are in dead-end corporate jobs. And it is human nature to be loyal to managers and organizations that sincerely care about you and invest in your long-term well-being. Despite what many economists preach about profit maximizing individuals, there is a growing body of evidence proving that purpose, mastery, and professional opportunities are important motivators, and people prefer to work in an environment where they can experience purpose and mastery of their own careers. Thus, many of your best employees will decide to stay with your organization out of loyalty to you, their empathetic manager who gave them the opportunities to grow professionally. But even more important is the reputation effect that your company will develop as you invest in each employee so that everyone's potential can be reached. The bottom line is quality people desire to grow professionally and are attracted to organizations in which they have opportunities to reach their potential.

CONCLUSION

As you'll recall, the ultimate purpose of empathy-based management is to enable your organization to grow and thrive in any business climate. Your organization's ability to prosper requires an effective response to each new challenge. For your organization to continuously solve each new problem that arises, you will need employees who are motivated to problem solve and create innovative solutions to each new problem as your organization changes. In order to meet this end goal of innovative and motivated employees, you as the manager must first meet the three intermediate goals of empathy-based management: to create an emotionally secure work environment, to give each employee hope, and to help each employee grow personally and professionally.

Chapters 3 and 4 teach you how to foster empathy around the problems and experiences of your employees. But I need to draw a distinction here. Chapter 3 is designed to help you empathize with your employee when he is in the middle of a crisis, and can help you reach your employee even when he is very emotionally upset. Chapter 4 gives you tools to help empathize on an everyday basis. For your average employee, most days at work may border on the mundane or even boring, rather than a crisis. On these days, empathy is important for each employee to feel your presence, support, and encouragement. It is also important to empathize with each of your employees on a daily basis in order to strengthen your relations, and also understand each person's state of mind. This becomes very useful for proactively problem solving, rather than responding reactively in your organization.

3

EMPATHIZING WITH EMPLOYEES DURING TIMES OF CRISIS

*Self-image sets the boundaries
of individual accomplishment.*
—MAXWELL MALTZ

*As a man changes his own nature, so does the
attitude of the world change towards him.*
—MAHATMA GANDHI

In order for any relationship to last, there is an underlying fundamental need for all parties to be accepted and understood. These are two of the goals all human beings seek when we enter into any relationship, including our work and professional relationships. This understanding is often overlooked by traditional management practices, but it is the starting point for empathy-based management.

As a manager, how can you reach out in a truly empathetic manner so that your employees will feel an authentic connection with you (rather than unintentionally saying inappropriate words and creating misunderstandings)?

In this chapter you will learn how to display empathetic behavior and convey unconditional acceptance and understanding with each employee when it is most needed, namely in the middle of difficult times in their lives, when they are looking to you for support and encouragement.

THE COGNITIVE AND THE EMOTIONAL REGIONS OF THE HUMAN BRAIN

Before we take a closer look at how to empathize with employees, it's important to review why we do what we do.

Human behavior is driven by both thoughts and feelings, and significantly different behavior will result depending on whether the body is responding to thoughts or feelings. As discussed in chapter 1, once the limbic region, or emotional portion of the brain, is triggered—particularly by such strong negative emotions as fear, anger, and frustration—stress hormones are released, and the cognitive portion of the brain shuts down. In other words, the person stops thinking and responds on instincts. This physiological behavior is known as a stress response to a stimulus, also called a fight-or-flight response. Picture someone going for a walk, and a very large dog barks wildly at the fellow as he passes by. All of a sudden the dog's chain snaps, and it races toward the walker, growling menacingly. At this point the amygdala in the poor fellow's brain is triggered, and he immediately behaves on instinct, either standing his ground (fight) or turning to run in fear (flight). Until he is able to escape harm, all behavior is emotional and instinctual; he devotes no time to logical thought. He simply can't until he is safe.

The same physiological processes also occur in the workplace. For example, suppose that an employee breaks a company policy and, as a result, the manager becomes emotional and harshly reprimands her. She will most likely feel threatened (an emotional response) by the manager's verbal attack, and a stress response will consume her brain. She will become defensive and angry—a response based on emotion rather than sound reasoning. The employee's angry response perpetuates the cycle, further triggering the amygdala in the manager's brain. With both limbic regions triggered, the manager and the employee stop thinking and act solely on impulse. Any decisions are made on emotion rather than logic.

It is critical that both the manager and the employee in this situation understand that their emotions can override their logic and thus influence their behaviors and hinder sound decision making. Otherwise, the manager could become emotional to the point of terminating the employee. This is obviously counterproductive in light of management's goal to motivate the employee to change her behavior and become more productive. (Note: This is why empathy-based management never uses punishment. Instead, it uses empathy and consequences when addressing employee behavioral issues. Punishment comes from another person; consequences are learned within oneself. Chapter 4 will explain the concept of consequences in detail.)

The manager who exercises empathy-based management wants to see the employee engage the cognitive portion of her brain and will therefore behave in ways that have a calming effect on the limbic region of the employee's brain (whenever the emotional environment becomes negative), so that the employee can once again think rationally in order to problem solve or make behavior changes.

ONE'S ABILITY TO SELF-REGULATE EMOTIONS VARIES FROM PERSON TO PERSON

It is important to note that each employee's ability to regulate their emotions will vary widely from person to person. Some employees, who grew up in stable families, will have steady and positive emotional outlooks on life. While other employees, who had more dysfunctional childhoods, may display a wide variety of emotional issues that can result in lowered worker productivity, including moodiness, impulse control, bitterness, anxiety, and depression.

Each time one of your employees experiences a strong negative emotional state, including fear, anger, shame, humiliation, or depression, your presence as an empathetic manager is beneficial in helping your employee begin to self-regulate his emotional states. Over time, in the presence of both an emotionally safe work environment and an empathetic manager who can help calm down the worker's emotions through supportive intersubjective experiences, your employee will become better able to self-regulate his emotional states.

INTERSUBJECTIVITY

When a manager and an employee share the same emotional response to an event—or, more precisely, the employee's *perception* of the event—this shared emotional experience is known as an intersubjective experience. *Inter* means between two or more people; *subjective* refers to a personal point of view. I've built my empathy-based management approach on the theory of intersubjectivity pioneered by Dr. Daniel Hughes, a clinical psychologist, and Dr. John Bowlby, a well-respected psychologist and pioneer researcher of the role of empathy in healthy childhood development. (For those interested in a deeper understanding of intersubjectivity theory, I suggest reading Hughes's book *Attachment-Focused Family Therapy* and Bowlby's book *A Secure Base*.)

Hughes explains the concept of intersubjectivity this way:

> Through intersubjective experience we become more able to identify, regulate, and express our affective life. Through such experiences, we are able to develop empathy for others and to successfully engage in shared, reciprocal, social experiences. Through

intersubjectivity we are able to understand the thoughts, wishes, and intentions of others just as we become able to identify and express our own. The inner lives of others become a central part of our own inner life. We are able to share our inner worlds, thus making our subjective worlds much more vital and interesting as well as making it possible for us to relate effectively within and about these worlds.[25]

Some people are better able to regulate or control their emotions, while others are less able. But for all of us, during times of stress, worry, fear, or outside pressures, we can enter into a mental state where we are all-consumed with our problem. The fight-or-flight response overtakes our rational mind. The idea behind an intersubjective experience is that the manager, who is in a calm (or normal) state of mind, interacts with an emotionally distressed employee. During their interaction, their emotional states begin to become unified, and the calm and controlled emotional state of the manager begins to influence and stabilize the employee's emotions.

During moments of intersubjectivity, according to Hughes, these behaviors occur:

The [manager]'s central intention is to focus on the experience of [the employee]. Her affect, attention, and intentions are fully engaged with [the employee].

The [manager] resonates with the initiatives and responses of her [employee].

The [manager], by resonating with her [employee's] vitality affect, is able to coregulate her [employee's] affective state.

The [manager] maintains an accepting, curious, and empathic affective/reflective state directed toward the subjective experience of her [employee].

> The [manager] actively accepts her [employee's] current functioning
> while encouraging her [employee] to take the next step in mastering
> his or her [professional] skills.[26]

According to Hughes, it is the manager's empathy, understanding, and concern for the employee's bad experience that joins their emotions and understanding together in an intersubjective experience. During an intersubjective experience facilitated by an empathetic manager, the employee is able to share his problem with less hesitation due to fear of possible rejection or shame. Over time, through intersubjective experiences to varying degrees, your employees will become more aware of and better able to self-regulate their emotions. You can learn to foster these successful experiences and help your employees calm their emotions as needed.

Three Requirements for Intersubjectivity

You might be scratching your head about now, wondering what all of this talk means and how you go about implementing empathy-based management on the job. Three requirements need to be met for an intersubjective experience to occur: congruent intentions, matched affect, and joint attention.

Requirement 1: Congruent Intentions

First, as a manager you will need to communicate that your intentions to help are congruent with your employee's concerns. The word *congruent* is simply a fancy way of saying compatible, or being in agreement, or in harmony. A good example of congruent intentions would be between two musicians in an orchestra. They have congruent intentions to play each song together in harmony. Their synchronized performance is a result of congruent intentions. Likewise, as a manager, you must express congruent intentions in order to reach out to your employee, namely a desire to solve a problem or provide help and support during a difficult experience.

It is crucial that you always have your employee's best interest in mind. Based on your communicated intentions, both in words and nonverbal behavior, your employee will decide whether or not to participate in an intersubjective experience with you.

Requirement 2: Matched Affect

The word *affect* refers to one's mental impression or feelings. The term *matched affect* means two people displaying identical emotions. If one person is angry, sad, or excited about an experience, the other person also becomes angry, sad, or excited as a result of hearing about the experience.

For matched affect to occur, you, the manager, must correctly interpret your employee's emotional state and match her emotions. The manager is required to enter into the employee's emotional state; the intersubjective experience will not occur if you are unwilling to match your employee's emotions.

Second, the manager does not try to use reason and talk the employee out of the emotions that the person is currently experiencing, be it anger, hurt, pain, frustration, sadness, excitement, etc. For example, if an employee has just finished a phone call with the police during which she learned that her son has been arrested for underage consumption of alcohol, the manager should not respond by saying: "Boys will be boys. It's not a big deal." To do so would deny the employee of the emotions that she is experiencing.

Instead, the manager matches the emotional state (or affect) of the employee.

For example, "Oh my goodness! I understand why you are so upset." The matched affect validates the employee's emotions and is required for your employee to be willing to enter into an intersubjective experience with you, the manager. Without matched affect, your employee will feel alone and misunderstood while experiencing intense emotions.

Before I go further, I'd like to take a minute to introduce you to the characters who appear in the scenarios in this and later chapters. The manager is Jesse, who is young, ambitious, reasonable, and trying to be a good supervisor. The employee is Pat, a seasoned worker in Jesse's department. Both names are intentionally gender neutral because with empathy-based management, one's gender does not matter (men as well as women can develop their ability to empathize); what matters is the well-being of every person in your organization.

For example, Pat has just learned that his son has been in a car accident. Jesse should not respond by saying: "Cheer up, Pat. Things will get better. Time heals all wounds." Rather, Jesse should respond by honoring or matching Pat's emotional state. For example, "Oh, no! Pat, what a horrible thing to have happened. I understand why you are so upset." This is an example of matched affect, when Pat's emotions become validated by Jesse's response. It is the starting point for an intersubjective experience to occur.

Requirement 3: Joint Attention

The third requirement for an intersubjective experience to occur is joint attention. The manager's attention, or focus, should not be on the event that the employee experienced but on the employee's perception or interpretation of the event.

For example, if Pat continues, "They said my son is okay, but they have taken him to the hospital to do a routine, precautionary exam," Jesse should not respond, "Did he have insurance? How much damage was done to your car?" This is the wrong focus. Instead Jesse needs to focus on Pat's son. A more empathetic response would be: "If you need or want to go to the hospital, go ahead and punch out. But please give me a call on my cell phone when you have time. I would also like to know how he is doing. Pat, I will be keeping your son in my thoughts and prayers."

Every event will elicit as many viewpoints as participants and witnesses. What matters for an intersubjective experience to occur is for the manager to enter into the employee's understanding of the event.

Continuing our example, Pat calls Jesse from the hospital: "Hi, Jesse. This is Pat. My son checked out OK. He was stopped at a stoplight when his car was rear-ended by a girl in high school who was texting on her phone. Fortunately, they said his headrest saved him from whiplash. Still, they wanted to do a precautionary exam to make sure he wasn't in danger."

An appropriate response from Jesse would be something like, "Wow, Pat, I bet you are relieved, and I am also relieved. I am glad to hear he is doing fine and that the accident was not his fault."

What matters is not the event itself but the employee's perception of the event. For you to be perceived as empathetic, you must confirm your employee's interpretation of the event. You can disagree with this interpretation but not before an intersubjective experience occurs. Otherwise the experience will not occur, and you will be perceived as judgmental and nonempathetic. We will talk more about this later in this chapter.

Well-known psychiatrist Dr. Daniel Amen explains the power of perception in this way:

> Our perceptions bear witness to our state of mind and the state of our brain. A calm . . . emotional brain leads to more rational thought; an overactive [emotional] brain is associated with greater anxiety and sadness . . . It is how your brain perceives situations, rather than the actual situations themselves, that causes you to react. I often write this equation for my patients: $A + B = C$ . . . where: A is the actual event, B is how we interpret or perceive the event, and C is how we react to the event.[27]

When the manager is open, nonjudgmental, and curious in regard to the employee's interpretation of an event, she and her employee are able to discuss the event in detail. During this discussion, first the manager seeks to understand the employee's perception and then together the manager and employee enter into an intersubjective experience in order to more fully explore and understand the event or problem.

THE FIVE STEPS OF THE INTERSUBJECTIVE EXPERIENCE

As you may know too well, one of the most challenging aspects of being a manager is dealing with people, particularly people who are emotionally upset. The purpose of creating an intersubjective experience is to deal with your employees when they become emotional—to help them calm down without becoming upset or emotional yourself. Following the five steps sequentially will help you guide them through discovery to understanding of their experiences and solutions to their problems. If you do not follow the steps sequentially, you may lose your employee's trust and she will not feel understood during every step in the process. Once your employee no longer feels understood, the intersubjective experience is prematurely cut short, and the desired results will not be realized.

Step 1: Comprehend Your Employee's Experience

As mentioned, the key to creating an intersubjective experience is to recognize the difference between the event and the employee's interpretation of the event. The focus of the intersubjective experience must be on the employee's interpretation and not the event itself. The event itself does not matter. The reason the employee's amygdala has triggered an intense emotional reaction is because of the perceived threat in the employee's interpretation of "what just happened." Thus, your focus must be on your employee's perspective and emotional reaction rather than on the facts of the event.

In step 1, ask questions in order to probe into your employee's interpretation of the event and actively listen as your employee explains his interpretation of the event. If your employee is too upset to explain his interpretation of the event, step 1 may require you to stop asking questions, pause, and help your employee calm down by using a calm voice and body language that communicates patience, understanding, and unconditional acceptance. You may need to give your employee time to calm down. This is normal. In the case of a very upset employee, patience is required in order to hear your employee's perception of his experience. As your employee shares his experience, listen closely to what is being said and watch body language for clues in order to fully comprehend your employee's understanding of the experience. For example, once your employee has calmed down enough to speak, is your employee clenching his fists or jaw, frowning, glaring, or breathing deeply? Then he may be very angry or upset. Is your employee tightening his body into a closed position? Then he may be afraid or fearful. Is your employee staring at the ground or refusing to make eye contact with you? Then he may be experiencing shame.

Step 2: Respond with Empathy, Understanding, and Acceptance

Once you understand the employee's interpretation of the event, respond to your employee with empathy, understanding, and acceptance. It is important that you do not skip step 2 before proceeding to step 3. Otherwise, your employee may not feel either understood or accepted and will not proceed to step 3 of the intersubjective experience.

It is of utmost importance that in step 1 and step 2 you make no judgment regarding your employee's experience of the event. Unconditionally accept your employee's account of the experience as he explains it. Meet the employee's interpretation of the event with your undivided attention and nonjudgmental curiosity. Your intention is to fully understand the employee's perspective of the event. And with this mindset, there is no need for your employee to defend his interpretation of the event, providing your employee an opportunity to fully explore the event with you. This opportunity is the primary objective of steps 1 and 2 of the intersubjective experience. As a manager, the intersubjective experience is also very beneficial because it allows you to fully comprehend both your employee's mindset and the internal relationships within your department.

Step 3: Investigate the Causes of the Event

After responding with empathy to your employee's personal interpretation of the event, the next step is for you to investigate the motives your employee attributes to the person(s) who caused the event. For example, your employee might say: "That other employee keeps picking on me because . . . she is jealous; she hates me; or, I won't join her little clique; etc." In step 3, you are trying to discover why your employee thinks the other employee acted the way he did, or other causes of the problem.

Step 3 requires you to ask questions in order to probe into your employee's attribution of motives behind the behavior of everyone involved in the event. It will require further active listening as your employee explains why she thinks people acted the way they did. Again, if your employee becomes too upset to formulate words in order to explain what she thinks, step 3 may require you to help the employee calm down by using a calm voice and displaying body language that communicates patience, understanding, and acceptance.

Step 4: Respond Again with Empathy, Understanding, and Acceptance

Once you fully comprehend your employee's interpretation of the motives behind the behavior of everyone involved in the event, respond to your employee with empathy, understanding, and unconditional acceptance. It can be a very intense emotional experience for your employee to explain the reason(s) behind the behavior that caused the event. At this point your employee may be emotionally and mentally tired. Again, it is important to not skip replying with empathy and understanding because at this point your employee will need some emotional reassurance. For example, respond with empathetic words such as: "Now I understand why you are so upset. You believe the other employee is trying to take your job . . . what a horrible realization. Wow! If someone tried to steal my job, I would be furious."

For the astute reader, in step 4 you are displaying the same behavior, namely an empathetic response, as in step 2. At this point it might be useful to summarize steps 1 through 4.

Step 1: Your employee explains the problem to you. Your focus is on your employee's perspective of the experience.

Step2: You respond with empathy, understanding, and unconditional acceptance.

Step 3: Your employee explains why the problem occurred, from her perspective.

Step 4: Again, you respond with empathy, understanding, and unconditional acceptance.

One Word of Warning

Your employee's explanation of the events of an incident and the motives behind everyone involved may become a very delicate matter for you to handle correctly. If your employee feels either misunderstood or unaccepted, this intersubjective experience will fail, and it may also be the end of any meaningful relationship between you and your employee. In other words, your employee may feel that his trust has been broken. Your employee may never again willingly share emotionally vulnerable concerns with you.

But if the employee feels understood and accepted during this time of emotional vulnerability, he will realize that you are a safe person who understands his concerns and is trustworthy. Also, with you being the supervisor, your department becomes an emotionally safe work environment for all of your employees. With an emotionally safe work environment, employees have an opportunity to fully utilize their talents for their work rather than taxing emotional energy preoccupied with being on guard while in the presence of one's supervisor.

Also, when the employee feels understood and accepted as she shares deeply emotional issues, the limbic region in her brain calms down. This is the point where a positive, productive, and loyal relationship begins.

Step 5: Cocreating New Meaning to the Incident and Finding Resolution

Your empathetic response in step 4 creates an emotionally safe and accepting environment in which you can further understand the incident. Your employee will then have an opportunity to discuss the incident in detail with you. Together, through back and forth dialogue, you and your employee bring new insights and further refine each other's understanding of the event. You now have the opportunity to clarify his interpretation of the incident from your point of view. We call this the cocreation of new meaning(s) of the event.

Continuing the example, it may be reasonable to say something to the effect of: "That must have been a horrible realization that the reason she is picking on you is because she wants your job. But actually from my perspective as manager, you are not in danger of losing your job. Do you realize you are one of the hardest-working employees in my department? Your evaluations have been consistently strong. As long as you want your job and you continue working hard, it is your job to keep. Have you thought about why she wants your job? Is this about her wanting your job, or more about her being dissatisfied with her own job?"

Once you both reach a more comprehensive and satisfactory understanding of the event, your employee may appreciate your insights and understanding as to why the event occurred, or she may desire a reasonable resolution to the event in order to create closure to the experience.

This is the end of the intersubjective experience. Your employee should leave the experience with three important reassurances: (1) a better understanding of why the event occurred; (2) having experienced her manager's empathy, understanding, and unconditional acceptance; and (3) some sort of closure to the event or problem.

An Example of an Intersubjective Experience

In the following example, Pat and Jesse share an intersubjective experience. Note how the five steps are used in order.

Pat: Can I have a minute of your time?

Jesse: Sure.

Pat: I can't stand being around Britney; she always gives me dirty looks. Whenever I say something, she always rolls her eyes. She is so mean. (Step 1)

Jesse: Her behavior sounds quite inappropriate to me. Whenever someone gives me a dirty look, I always wonder if I did something wrong. (Step 2)

Pat: At first I did the same thing. I wondered what I did wrong; now I just get angry every time it happens.

Jesse: Pat, I appreciate you not retaliating, and I also appreciate you sharing this with me. I was not aware that this behavior was occurring. Do you have any idea why she might be giving you dirty looks? (Step 3)

Pat: Well, I don't know for sure, but it started when you decided to have me run our company's booth at the state fair. I am guessing Britney wanted to go to the fair. Ever since I have returned, her attitude toward me has changed.

Jesse: That is truly sad. It sounds very petty on Britney's behalf. If she wanted to go to the state fair, she should have just asked; we could have made room for her." (Step 4) "Did Britney ask if she could go with you to the fair?

Pat: Well . . . actually . . . she did ask, but I told her there wasn't room. (Start of step 5)

Jesse: Pat, thank you for your honesty. I think you may be correct in your assessment of why she is upset with you. Britney may be upset, but that does not excuse her inappropriate behavior.

Pat: Definitely not.

Jesse: So, what would you like me to do? Would you like me to talk with her, or would you prefer to have a group meeting?

Pat: I don't know. I would just like her bad attitude toward me to stop.

Jesse: Might I make a suggestion? I will watch for her attitude, and if I see it occur, I will confront it. OK? A bad attitude is counterproductive to everyone's motivation and can be contagious. But I do believe there is a deeper issue here. I think all of us, myself included, need to work on our communication skills.

Pat: Sounds good.

In this example Jesse guides Pat through the five steps of the intersubjective experience. Note that as Jesse does not blame Pat for his interpersonal trouble with Britney, Pat feels safe enough to be honest regarding his treatment of Britney. Through intersubjectivity, Jesse is able to uncover a core cause of the problem between these two employees, and Pat leaves with a reassurance that the problem will be addressed.

SIX IMPORTANT NOTES REGARDING
INTERSUBJECTIVE EXPERIENCES

1. Throughout the intersubjective experience, it is very important to give your employee's brain time to think. As your employee's emotions start calming down, the cognitive portion of his brain will begin to function normally once again. His brain will have an opportunity to think rationally once again, but it will require time to understand and process new ideas and interpretations.

2. In step 5, rather than telling your employee what you think, instead, using a curious tone of voice, ask your employee questions for clarification. This may be a more effective way to help your employee discover deeper meanings into why the event occurred—deeper than her original impressions. The best way for each of us to learn, with the greatest comprehension, is self-discovery, rather than secondhand, by someone telling you a new piece of knowledge.

3. In the case of misconduct on behalf of your employee, cocreating new meaning during an intersubjective experience does not excuse the employee's behavior. The employee is still responsible for his behavior and must face the natural consequences of his misconduct. The consequences to your employee's misconduct may create closure to the intersubjective experience.

4. When discussing another employee while cocreating a new meaning of any event, it is very important that you do not break confidentiality regarding other employees. For example, the reason the other person may seem to want this employee's job is because the other person has mental health issues and forgot to take his medicine yesterday. As a result, he was rude to everyone. Or, the other employee may have been told yesterday that his position was going to be eliminated from the company. Even though as manager you may know this to be true, you may not be able to share this confidential information with your

employee while cocreating new meaning during the intersubjective experience.

5. Creating closure to an event is very important to both the employee and your organization, because with closure, your employee can stop dwelling on the event and start focusing on the tasks at hand with her job.

6. It is especially important to never shame your employee during an intersubjective experience.

For all of us, at any age, shame is too difficult and devastating to experience, especially in the presence of one's supervisor. As you read in chapter 1, the limbic region perceives experiencing a shaming event to be life threatening and shuts down both our neocortex and the limbic region, and all thinking and emotions in our brain stop. We simply feel numb, and we have an all-consuming desire to either hide or run away.

According to Gershen Kaufman, "Shame is loss of face, . . . [and if] unchecked, shame can engulf the self, immersing the individual deeper into despair. To live with shame is to feel alienated and defeated, never quite good enough to belong."[28] If an employee feels shamed, his only impulse will be to leave as quickly as possible and, hopefully, never see you again. And the employee will then loathe you as long as he works for your organization.

BENEFICIAL RESULTS FROM INTERSUBJECTVITY

One of the primary emotional results of intersubjectivity is that through your words, receptive listening, tone of voice, and body language, you can achieve the first goal of empathy-based management: to create an emotionally safe environment. You will need to consistently display these same behaviors every day, during the private type of emotional exchanges described above and throughout ordinary workday interactions.

Second, through the intersubjective experience, your employee should realize three important reassurances: (1) a better intuition into the causes of the event; (2) the manager's empathy, understanding, and support; and (3) some sort of closure to the experience. These three realizations not only create closure to a bad experience in the mind of your employee, they also create hope for a better future. Giving your employees hope is the second goal of empathy-based management.

Likewise, intersubjective experiences help your employee to start to grow both personally and professionally—the third goal of empathy-based management. When your employee knows she has the understanding, acceptance, and empathy of her manager, it has a calming effect on the limbic region in her brain. Therefore she can stop being preoccupied by emotions and start thinking; problem solving becomes both possible and much less laborious. Intersubjective experiences influence the employee's self-efficacy, the belief in one's own ability to succeed at tasks and reach goals. As self-efficacy rises, so does the worker's drive, goals, and ambitions in life.

CONCLUSION

Chapter 3 provided tools to help you empathize with an employee when he is experiencing a crisis. The core instrument you can use to reach out to an employee who is emotionally upset is the intersubjective experience. Guiding your employee through the five steps of the intersubjective experience, you can give your employee the gifts of better understanding the experience and the opportunity to experience closure to an emotionally charged event. Your employee will leave feeling your empathy and unconditional acceptance and support.

In chapter 4, you will learn how to use tools to help you become more empathetic on an everyday basis.

4

TOOLS MANAGERS CAN USE FOR EVERYDAY EMPATHY-BASED MANAGEMENT

Some pursue happiness; others create it.
—ANONYMOUS

Happiness is not the absence of conflict,
but the ability to cope with it.
—ANONYMOUS

The purpose of this chapter is to give you a practical guide on how to become more empathetic in your everyday style of management. The good news is that although some people are naturally more empathetic, empathy does not depend on your personality. All of us, with training, can learn to be more empathetic. Ultimately, your manifestation of empathy will reflect your personality. It matters not whether you have a very charismatic personality or are just an ordinary person with a self-perceived "boring" personality; with practice you will become a very interesting and caring manager whom all of your employees hold in high regard, resulting from your ability to empathize. It takes practice and hard work, but every one of us is capable of becoming more empathetic, if we choose to do so.

The first half of this chapter is a practical guide on how to empathize in a workplace setting. The topics covered are how to: (1) figure out your employee's emotional state; (2) join your employee in her emotional state; (3) choose the correct words in order to convey empathy; (4) read your employee's nonverbal communications; and (5) convey empathetic nonverbal body language.

The purpose of the second half of the chapter is to clarify what is and what is not empathetic behavior by explaining seven pitfalls to avoid while attempting to become more empathetic in your management practices.

The contents of this chapter are intended to be a guide on how to empathize with your employees on a daily basis, when there is no immediate crisis. But, if at any time while interacting with your employee, you realize something is bothering your employee—or the amygdala in your employee's brain has been triggered—you should proceed to enter an intersubjective experience with your employee as explained in chapter 3.

HOW TO EMPATHIZE IN THE WORKPLACE SETTING

I am often asked the question, "Management based on empathy sounds like a good idea, but exactly how does a person become more empathetic?" This is an excellent question because the devil is always in the details. There is no one correct manifestation of empathy; how each manager expresses empathy will depend on her personality. The key to empathetic behavior is not what you say but rather the manner in which you say it. Your tone of voice and body language, rather than the actual words you speak, will determine if you are perceived as being empathetic.

There are two parts to becoming a more empathetic manager. First, every day when you arrive at work, you will need to figure out the emotional state of each employee. Second, you will need to join each employee in his or her emotional state. Instructions for both steps will now be explained in detail.

Determine the Employee's Emotional State

The first and most important rule to figuring out your employee's emotional state is to *never* ask the question, "How are you feeling?" You'll encounter many employees who either don't know what they are feeling or don't know how to verbalize it. Let us return to our friends Jesse and Pat.

Jesse: Good morning. How are you doing?

Pat: Good.

Jesse: What do you mean by good?

Pat: I don't know; I am fine.

Jesse: What do you mean by fine?

Pat: I don't know, but actually I changed my mind. I'm starting to feel irritated because you keep asking me all of these annoying questions.

Unfortunately, using the above line of questioning, Jesse cannot hope to uncover Pat's true emotional state.

Here's a *better way* to approach your employee: Rather than asking, "How are you doing?" which is a very personal question, ask, "How are things going today?" or "What is the weather forecast for your work today?" or "Is our department hitting home runs, getting on base, or striking out today?"

All of these questions focus on events, rather than the state of one's self. People can give reasons better than they can explain emotions. Most people are not good at explaining or sharing their own emotions. But if everything is going well or normal, people will let you know. On the other hand, if there is a problem, though they may not be able to share their internal emotional state; they will likely be willing to share what the problem is so that you can resolve it. As they describe the problem that is being faced, their disposition, body language, and tone of voice will reflect their emotional state.

Here is an example of a more fruitful approach Jesse might take to find out how Pat is doing today.

Jesse: Good morning, Pat. How is everything going today?

Pat: Good.

Jesse: Good, are there any new problems?

Pat: Nope.

Jesse: Good, I am glad to hear things are going well this morning.

Pat: Thanks.

In this example, things are going well for Pat. Jesse has made a brief but important connection. Pat knows that Jesse cares. This is important. And thus, this is all the interaction that is required for Jesse today.

As a manager, there is no need to go out of your way to find out each employee's emotional state. This may actually be perceived as artificial and a bit overdone. But over the course of each workday, if you notice an employee not behaving as his normal self, it is important to stop and take a moment to inquire how things are going.

A Better Way to Show Your Employee Empathy

And here's an even *better way* to show empathy: Get to know your employee well enough so that you can sense when a variation in the person's nonverbal behavior is signaling a change from his normal emotional state.

As Jesse builds a personal relationship with Pat and builds on it on a daily basis, they start to develop greater comprehension of each other's thoughts and emotions.

Jesse: Morning, Pat. What's the score today?

Pat: Morning, Jesse. Yesterday was all double bogies; today is par with a few birdies.

This is all the communication that Jesse needs to undertake. Jesse built upon his previous knowledge of Pat's love of golf to inquire how Pat was doing.

By Pat's answer, it is obvious he is doing much better today than yesterday.

UNDERSTANDING YOUR EMPLOYEES' EMOTIONS/FEELINGS

In order to develop a personal relationship with your employees, find out their hobbies or passions and initiate an ongoing dialogue about these interests. For example, if an employee is an avid sports fan with a favorite team, keep a game schedule in your office. If you are not a sports fan, just watch game highlights on ESPN, the local news, or the Internet. Each day read the game highlights from the night before so you are able to talk about a topic that the employee enjoys. The following steps illustrate this approach.

Step 1

When you interact with your employee for the first time, make a comment such as: "What are your thoughts on the game last night?"; "Wow, all I can say is wow! Did you see the game last night?"; or (take a big breath) "That was brutal last night"; or "Did you see that bad call? They were robbed last night!" If your employee's favorite team won, you could say, "I know, it was so much fun!" If the team lost, you could say, "That was painful"; "That game sucked."; or "We'll get them next time."

Step 2

Listen and watch. Listen to what your employee has to say and for voice inflections, and focus on your employee's body language. Once your employee picks up the conversation, it is critical that you stop talking and let him take control of the conversation. He will either change the conversation to what he wants to talk about, or he will let the conversation die.

Underlying this conversation is an opportunity for the employee to share more important issues that may be on his mind. Because your employee is already talking about a subject that he cares deeply about, it is relatively easy to switch the conversation to another topic that he is concerned about. All of us want to share the important moments in our life—good or bad—with someone, but we need to trust the person first.

If something important in the employee's life happened, he will share it with his manager if trust has been established. This is the point at which you, the manager, will find out what your employee is feeling emotionally. The employee may have something positive to share, such as, "My daughter's team just made the state tournament"; "I saw a good movie last night; it is worth seeing"; "I have a new idea for our office"; or "I found a new house; we made an offer this morning!"

He may have something negative to share: "My son crashed his bike last night and broke his arm"; "My baby still is up half the night every night"; or "My coworker is still being a jerk. He said some very mean things again today."

He may even have something work related to share: "I heard a rumor that . . . Is it true?"

Or he may end the conversation, which may occur for a variety of reasons: He may be a private person; he may have nothing newsworthy to talk about; or, he may need to focus on his work. If the employee needs to return to work, this is an excellent signal for both the manager and the employee. Also, it signals that the employee is committed, engaged, and focusing on the task at hand. In a few short moments, or even in a single gesture, you can make a connection with your employee. Build on this connection with your employee every day. As long as trust is not violated, over time the connection between the two of you will grow stronger and stronger.

If the employee wants to end the conversation, it is important not to push him to continue. Let the employee control the conversation. Every day the conversation must be natural, not forced or artificial.

So, at this point, there are two ways to understand the employee's emotional state. First, she may have told you verbally what is going on in her life. Or, second, her nonverbal body language and voice inflections clearly display her current mood. As manager, look for deviations in nonverbal behavior from your employee's normal disposition.

• • •

Final Note: If a company policy issue arises while visiting with the employee, always separate the person from the action. Affirm your employee, and address the behavior. Behavior must be confronted, for it is in the best interest of both the company and in helping the employee grow and mature both professionally and as a person.

JOIN YOUR EMPLOYEE IN HER EMOTIONAL STATE

After figuring out your employee's emotional state, the empathetic manager joins the employee in that emotional state. There are three parts to effectively display empathetic behavior that will be explained in this section: 1) prerequisites; 2) empathetic words; and 3) body language or nonverbal messages.

Prerequisites

To reiterate, the key to empathy is not what you say but the way you say it. You will need to have unconditional positive regard for your employee in order to effectively honor your employee's emotional state. Therefore, empathy requires you to monitor your tone of voice and body language at all times.

Beyond unconditional positive regard, there are four prerequisites to being empathetic, which you must understand and decide to do in order to be perceived as being empathetic around your employees.

Prerequisite #1: Practice Empathetic Behaviors

In their book *The Power of Empathy,* Ciaramicoli and Ketcham present eight empathetic behaviors. They also present the dark-side reflection of each empathetic behavior.

These dark-side reflections are the polar opposite attributes of empathetic behavior.

Empathic Behavior	Dark-Side Reflection
Honesty	Dishonesty, deception, deceit
Humility	Pride, conceit, egotism, arrogance
Acceptance	Perfectionism
Tolerance	Intolerance, bias, prejudice
Gratitude	Ingratitude, greed, thoughtlessness
Faith	Cynicism, suspicion, skepticism
Hope	Despair
Forgiveness	Resentment, bitterness, hatred[29]

Often in the business world we encounter people who embody the dark-side behavior rather than empathetic behavior. It may be a temptation for you to fall into dark-side reflections in order to either survive or succeed in corporate America today. Although it may be seductive, do not fall for the temptation. All of us have our shortcomings in our attitudes and attributes; that is human nature. But a person who consistently displays dark-side reflections will not be perceived as empathetic.

Even worse, as discussed in chapter 1, every one of us can sense other people's dispositions through the mirror neurons in our brain. Every one of your employees can tell if you have an empathetic disposition or a personality that reflects the dark side of human nature. The problem is that a person who displays dark-side attributes is consumed with one's self rather than being other-centered. No one wants to have a relationship with a person who displays dark-side-reflection attributes. But through an innate desire for belongingness, every human being desires to develop a relationship with another person who displays empathetic behaviors.

All of us display both empathetic and dark-side behaviors. But if your goal is to become a manager who is perceived as empathetic in order to create a relationship that gives your employees hope, helps them to grow, and, ultimately, is a foundation for motivation, make a conscious effort every day to choose behaviors that embody the nature of empathy. Let these empathetic behaviors guide your thoughts and actions, rather than the corresponding dark-side reflections.

Prerequisite #2: Interact on a Personal Level

You must not only display empathetic qualities; you must be willing to interact on a personal level with your employees as well. The empathetic manager enjoys the company of his employees and gets to understand their personalities and their idiosyncrasies. He gets to know their likes, dislikes, families, and hobbies. The manager is proud of each employee, and his pride is reflected in his words, intentions, and nonverbal cues. Your willingness to engage on a personal level is required if you are to respond in a way that honors your employee's emotional state. Employees cannot enter into a personal relationship with their manager if he is not willing to interact with them on a personal level.

It has been suggested that if a manager sets aside his formal disposition and develops a personal relationship with each employee, and each employee can see the manager's humanity—his strengths and weaknesses—the employees may consider the manager to be either weak or flawed. Paradoxically, the opposite is true. As the manager willingly gives his employees respect and control, he gains his employees' respect and loyalty. His employees look to him for his lead, direction, and insights. Through his personal connection, they willingly follow his lead.

Prerequisite #3: Your Actions and Intentions Need to Be Authentic

The empathetic manager needs to consider how all of his actions are perceived from his employee's point of view. This means giving your employee undivided attention.

Likewise, names are important. Get to know every employee's name or preferred nickname. It is fine and normal for the manager and employees to talk on a first-name basis. If an employee is required to address his manager by a title, rather than his first name, this creates a barrier to the employee having a personal relationship with his manager.

As stated, everyone is capable of empathy, and how expressions of empathy are manifested depend on personality. If a person is humorous, she may use humor in relating to people; serious, she may use facts to help empathize; logical, she will use reasoning to empathize, etc. But if your attempt to empathize does not match your personality, any attempt to empathize will be perceived by others as artificial and will fail for lack of authenticity.

Again, think through how your actions are perceived by others.

For example, the manager should not be a name-dropper around her employees. For example, "Yesterday I had lunch with Bill (Gates) and afterward I joined Barack (Obama) for a round of golf." This statement is a form of bragging and will ostracize your employees.

Prerequisite #4: High Expectations of Employees

The empathetic manager must have high expectations of all employees. This tells each of your employees that you believe in their ability. To have low expectations of an employee tells the employee that the manager does not believe in him, and this will kill any person's motivation.

Also, through neuroplasticity, the human brain can learn new tasks, and people can improve at any task, including problem solving, with practice. Therefore, in an emotionally safe environment, where the cognitive portion of our brains can mature and grow, every person in your organization can experience professional growth. But high expectations are a prerequisite for both professional growth and sustainable employee motivation.

Empathetic Words

For the manager who has figured out an employee's emotional state, the next step of empathizing with, or matching, this emotional state is a critical one. The words chosen by the manager must accomplish the task of conveying to the employee that the manager understands his emotional state and is joining his affective state.

For example, an employee might approach her manager at work and say, "John is not doing his work. Watch him. He holds his cell phone under his desk and spends most of the day texting." An empathetic response from the manager would be: "Oh no, it sounds like John and I need to have a private conversation" or "Thank you for bringing this to my attention." The manager is joining her subordinate in her emotional state.

Notice that an empathetic manager does not say, "Don't worry about him" or "Have *you* confronted John on his behavior?" Both of these statements would deny the employee of her feelings. Also, asking if the employee has confronted John on the issue may add additional stress on top of the anger and frustration she is already experiencing. The very fact that she has not confronted John on his behavior suggests that she may not be comfortable doing so.

After the employee shares the problem and the manager responds with empathy, stories can be an excellent resource to further strengthen the manager's empathetic behavior. For example, the manager may ask, "I had a very similar experience once. Would you mind if I shared what happened to me?" Sharing stories is a way to further demonstrate the manager's empathy and build a connection because the employee learns that he is not alone in his experience. A manager sharing his own personal feelings about his own performance or unfortunate experiences is a part of developing a personal relationship.

After the employee feels the manager has joined her in her emotional state and the employee is ready to listen to the manager, it may be useful for the manager to also affirm the employee. For example, if confronting a behavior issue, the manager might say something like: "I know you. You're smart and you learn from these experiences." This statement reinforces in the employee's brain the understanding that "I am capable" and that my manager also recognizes this. Even though the exchange may be confrontational, affirming the employee while confronting the behavior creates trust between both parties, who both end up feeling respected after their interaction.

A Workplace Example of Not Denying the Employee's Feelings

To reiterate, the key to making empathy-based management work is to first understand the emotional state of the other person. Only after you understand the other person's emotional state can you make an appropriate response.

In this example, I will contrast an unempathetic response that denies the employee's feelings with an empathetic response that validates the employee's feelings.

The dismissive/unempathetic response:

Lisa (employee): Can I have a minute of your time?

Jesse: Sure.

Lisa: Can I have the first week of December off? I need to study for final exams.

Jesse: Can you finish the project you're working on before you take a week off?

Lisa: It will be a lot of work, but . . . yes, I can get it finished.

Jesse: If you get your project finished, you may have the week off. How do your final exams look?

Lisa: Good, except for algebra. I am not doing too well in the class right now.

Jesse: You know what? Don't worry about it. You'll do fine. You are a very intelligent person. You will ace all of your final exams.

At this point, not only has Jesse failed to empathize but also has denied Lisa of her feelings. If Lisa is having problems with algebra, she is anxious about the upcoming final exam. Jesse's denying Lisa of her feelings makes her feel alone and misunderstood, which can create more anxiety in the limbic region of her brain. Unintentionally, Jesse's comments created a psychological break in their relationship when Lisa feels alone and misunderstood.

Contrast these results with the following more empathetic response:

Lisa: Can I have a minute of your time?

Jesse: Sure.

Lisa: Can I have the first week of December off? I need to study for final exams.

Jesse: Can you finish the project you are working on before you take a week off?

Lisa: It will be a lot of work, but . . . yes, I can get it finished.

Jesse: If you get your project finished, you may have the week off. How do your final exams look?

Lisa: Good, except for algebra. I am not doing too well in the class right now.

Jesse: Yes, you know . . . math can be very frustrating. The toughest classes I had in high school were my math classes. Did you know that I almost failed my accounting class in high school? Even to this day I am fine until I get to credits and debits. I always get debits and credits mixed up. I almost quit college when I found out that I was required to take an accounting class. But then I found a good accounting tutor, and we met each week during the entire semester. He helped me understand debits and credits. Do you think a tutor might help you with algebra?

Lisa: Umm . . . umm. See, here is the problem . . . it is really embarrassing. I don't want anyone to find out—

Jesse: Yeah, it is a horrible feeling. I never did tell my parents about accounting class. I don't want you to have to endure a similar bad experience. Would a tutor help, if we can arrange it so no one else needs to know?

Lisa: I am willing to try a tutor, but I don't make any promises that it will help.

At this point, through empathizing with Lisa's feelings of anxiety, shame, and inadequacy, Jesse has created a psychological connection with Lisa, giving her hope regarding her math problem. Lisa no longer feels alone in her problem, and she feels that Jesse, her manager, cares about her on a personal level. This personal understanding becomes a source of hope and loyalty toward Jesse. From loyalty comes both a personal association with and a desire to please Jesse. This is the starting point for sustainable motivation. Lisa will remain loyal to Jesse as long as Jesse continues to be empathetic; keeps words and actions consistent; and does not betray Lisa's trust.

Empathetic Words in Response to Your Employee's Emotional State

As you understand your employee's emotional state, it is important to use words that match that state of mind. The following examples illustrate how an empathetic manager might respond to thirty different commonplace human emotions.

Employee's Emotion	Manager's Empathetic Statement
Angry	"Wow, I would have come unglued if that had happened to me."
Ashamed	"I bet you wished you could become invisible."
Bored	"It would have been hard for me to not fall asleep."

Cautious	"I agree, that's a tough one. I just need some time to think about it."
Confident	"I have no doubt."
Confusion	"That doesn't make any sense."
Depressed	"Some days I hate getting out of bed in the morning."
Disgust	"How revolting; it makes me want to throw up."
Embarrassed	"I would have turned bright red if that had happened to me."
Excited	"I'm getting goose bumps just listening to you."
Exhausted	"Personally, when I don't get enough sleep, I get the worst headache."
Energized	"Go get 'em."
Fear	"Is the hair on the back of my neck standing up?"
Frightened	"Whoa! I would have freaked out."
Frustrated	"I bet you just want to bang your head against a wall."
Guilty	"That's the worst feeling in the whole world."
Happy	"Wonderful! That's awesome!"
Hopeful	"You know what? I've got a good feeling about this."

In love	"I'm very happy for both of you."
Jealous	"That doesn't sound fair to me."
Lonely	"Going home to an empty apartment is no fun."
Mischievous	"Uh-oh, they had better be paying attention."
Overwhelmed	"Wow, where do you even start?"
Nervous	"So, when did you figure out what happened?"
Shy	"Sometimes it's hard for me to start a conversation."
Surprised (positive)	"That's amazing! I don't know what to say."
Surprised (negative)	"Oh my goodness, that's horrible."
Sad	"I feel sad that this happened to you."
Suspicious	"A person needs to keep both eyes wide open around here."
Vulnerable	"I'm honored you made yourself vulnerable to share this with me."

Practice reading the above responses until you understand how each statement helps you join your employee in his emotional state. But remember, each statement must be honest and sincere in order to be believable. With this in mind, create your own empathetic response for each emotion—responses that match your personality. Practice saying your empathetic statement for each emotion until it becomes a natural response. Your empathetic response should sound natural and be a reflection of your personality. An effective manager is always ready with an empathetic response. With practice it will become second nature.

End with a Message of Hope

Anytime your employee shares a personal concern, always end your conversation with a message of hope. This message is to be delivered only after you have empathized with the emotional state of your employee. Your message of hope will not be heard until you have been perceived as responding empathetically to your employee's mood. Finally, if your employee already has a reasonable plan (already has hope), you may not be required to give a message of hope.

Here are three examples of ending with a message of hope: "What have we learned from what just happened?"; "What can we do different next time?"; and "What a mess . . . but I know you, you will get them next time."

Body Language or Nonverbal Messages

As mentioned, sometimes the better starting point for the manager to discover the employee's emotional state is to pick up on a person's nonverbal clues, which includes facial expressions and body language.

Conversation is 33 percent verbal and 67 percent nonverbal. A student once asked me a rather profound question: "Why is human conversation roughly a third verbal and two-thirds nonverbal behavior?" After much research, I have discovered the answer lies in the arrangement of our nervous system. The majority of information from the human brain travels through the nerves in the spinal cord to reach the body. There is one exception: cranial nerves originate directly from the brain. Two cranial nerves, responsible for

ACKNOWLEDGE YOUR OWN EMOTIONAL STATE

Initially, developing a personal relationship with each of your employees is a lot of hard work. It will continue to be emotionally laborious until trust has been established with each employee. After trust has been established, each relationship will still require work, but it will not be nearly as intense.

But even after establishing a relationship with each employee, participation in intersubjective experiences can be exhausting for either/both the manager and the employee because it requires you to use both your heart and mind. You will be required to focus on, and respond appropriately to, both your employee's train of thought and his emotional states. In order to facilitate an intersubjective experience, you must give your employee your undivided attention and communicate consistently—both verbally and nonverbally.

Understand that interacting with an employee in an intersubjective experience as well as just empathizing on a day-to-day basis will be emotionally draining on you. This is normal and to be expected. Therefore, it is important for you to assess your own emotional energy after each intersubjective experience. How is your level of emotional energy? If it is normal, go ahead and go back to work. On the other hand, if you realize you are emotionally drained, give yourself permission to take a break. Do some physical exercise, like taking your frustration or anxiety out in the weight room, or spend some time on the golf course and use your energy hitting golf balls, or go for a walk or a run to decompress. Or simply go out for lunch. But realize trying to immediately go back to work when you are emotionally exhausted is pointless. You will not be able to focus, and nothing productive will be accomplished until you give your brain a break in order to decompress.

vision and smell, go directly into the neocortex of your brain. The other ten emerge directly from your brain stem.

Perhaps because of their importance to human survival, the nerves for sight, hearing, and smell send information received from the environment around you directly to your brain. The other cranial nerves are responsible for eight important body functions: tone of voice, eye movement, facial muscles, head movement, shoulder position, heart rate, breathing, and swallowing. Because of their direct link to the human brain, these cranial nerves reflect the thoughts and feelings of the brain. Therefore, nonverbal behavior by these body gestures, including tone of voice, eye movements, facial muscles, and shoulder position, directly reflect the internal reactions of the brain.

Learning to read these nonverbal cues is like learning any language. For some people, reading body language is a learned skill, especially for those in law enforcement, the military, and professional poker players, as well as for people who grew up in unsafe homes or neighborhoods. For most of us, reading nonverbal cues comes through practice.

Likewise, for an empathetic manager to be trusted, your nonverbal message must be congruent with the words you are using. Nonverbal behavior is more important than a person's spoken words because nonverbal behavior conveys a person's intentions. In other words, it is not what the manager tells each employee; it is how he says it, including tone of voice and body language/stance and facial expression. As an empathetic manager, your nonverbal message must always express unconditional positive regard for each employee.

Unfortunately, because of the power of emotions occurring in the limbic region of the human brain, a manager cannot fake body language. It always reveals his mood and his intentions. If the manager is angry, apathetic, or uses a sarcastic tone of voice, the manager's nonverbal message will reflect his mood. Immediately the employee will respond to the manager's emotional state rather than the words he is speaking. In order to be empathetic it is important for you to be honest with yourself regarding your emotional state at all times.

If you are angry, sad, or embarrassed, be honest with yourself and guard your words carefully, for it is easy to say something that you might regret later. Realize that your emotional state of mind will affect both the words you choose and your tone of voice during interactions with anyone. Be aware that as a manager, and as a human being, you cannot fake body language regarding your true emotional state. Some managers are able to pretend quite well, but an empathetic employee will discern through their cover-up.

Nonverbal Behavior That Conveys Empathy

Whenever interacting with employees, the manager needs to self-monitor these six aspects of her nonverbal communication with regard to being empathetic:

1. Make eye contact, and keep eye contact during the entire conversation. It reveals that you are interested, giving your full attention, and trustworthy.

2. Get close to and touch (handshake and pat on the back) your employee to reveal how comfortable you are with the person. Empathy requires that the manager appears to feel comfortable with his employee. Some employees like to be touched; others do not. Respect the other person's wishes in this regard. If an employee appreciates your touch, it can be a source of connection, and it can convey your confidence in your worker.

3. Smile and lean forward as the employee speaks to show that you like the employee and are very interested in what she has to say. It is important for the manager to smile with both her mouth and her eyes. If she smiles with only her mouth, her eyes will betray her true feelings.

4. Do things with the employee outside of formal meetings to signal that you enjoy the presence of your employees. Some examples include: keep track of and bring a cake to celebrate each person's birthday; participate in a funny contest each week or an office fantasy football pool; eat lunch with your employees, whenever possible; spend some time helping employees with their work.

5. Provide some nonverbal "sugar"—always—whenever you interact with employees. This includes communicating that you are proud; being patient and understanding; sharing jokes and laughter; and providing an occasional positive surprise, such as homemade chocolate chip cookies or souvenirs from a business trip.

6. Laugh and be playful when matters are not serious. Enjoy both your life and your work, be curious and accepting of each employee, and entertain their ideas no matter how reasonable or foolish they may be. Create a work environment that is warm and inviting and safe and relaxed, yet creative and stimulating. Ultimately the work environment will reflect your personality, but create an atmosphere where everyone, no matter their personality or shortcomings, is accepted and engaged.

Display this same nonverbal empathetic behavior that reflects unconditional positive regard for the employee when you need to discuss a difficult or sensitive issue with an employee.

SEVEN PITFALLS TO AVOID AS YOU LEARN HOW TO EMPATHIZE

When I've visited with managers regarding the idea of empathy-based management, they often respond with a statement to the effect of, "Well, I am a very empathetic person. I care deeply about my employees." But when I interview the employees regarding their manager, I often hear a different story. "My manager is too focused on his own issues to truly care about us and our needs." Many managers really do care deeply about their employees, so this difference in perceptions is particularly unfortunate. But it has helped me to realize that I need to present not only what empathetic behavior looks like but also to explain a variety of behaviors that may seem to be empathetic, but they are perceived as being unempathetic. What follows is a description of seven common pitfalls that a manager must avoid in order to practice empathy-based management.

Pitfall #1: Nonempathetic Behavior

Although this has been mentioned previously, I believe this point is worth repeating because asking questions that are too personal is a common mistake people make when attempting to become more empathic, especially in regards to understanding another person's emotional state. In spite of the fact that empathy-based management's focus is on people's emotions, never ask an employee directly, "How did that make you feel?" People hate that question because it sounds like the manager is trying to analyze the employee. Also, without practice, most people are not very good at analyzing their own emotional states. Rather, in order to be empathetic, tell the person how the situation would make you feel if that happened to you. It will help them to explore their own emotions.

Also, never ask an employee to do something that you don't ask yourself to do. This creates a supervisor-subordinate mindset for both the manager and the employee.

Finally, when telling a story of your own experiences or emotional tribulations, in order to empathize, never brag. For example, don't say, "My problem was ten times harder than your problem." This will come across as the manager diminishing the other person's problem.

Pitfall #2: Punishment vs. Consequences

When employees are punished for violating a company policy or displaying inappropriate behavior in the workplace, it can lead them to direct their anger toward the manager who disciplines them. Employees can also become discouraged. As the employee's amygdala triggers a fight-or-flight response to the perceived punishment, all thinking will cease, and the brain will instead jump right to an emotional response (often a strong, negative one) along the brain's pathway toward action.

"I told you so" statements from the manager will likewise activate the limbic region of the employee's brain. Never say, "I tried to warn you, but you would not listen" or "I hope you learned your lesson." These statements, intentionally or unintentionally, shame the person and create a feeling of opposition rather than an emotional connection between people.

Likewise, any of the following behaviors will result in the employee not learning from the consequences of his actions:

- The manager explaining to the employee the lesson to be learned from the consequence.
- The manager's nonverbal behavior displaying either disgust or anger.
- The manager giving in to the employee's pleas to be given a warning, rather than being required to face the consequences of one's own action.
- The manager reminding the employee how many times the employee misbehaved.

All of these actions on behalf of the manager will prevent the employee from learning from the consequences of her behavior.

Contrasting punishment to consequences, punishment comes from the manager and will depend on the emotional state of the manager. Consequences are the natural result of one's action and are learned from inside of one's self. For a simple example of a consequence, if a person falls off a ladder, how badly one gets hurt will depend on the person's weight and how far one falls. This person will not need a lecture from a manager regarding this experience.

Employees do not want to be told correct answers; they want to think for themselves regarding any matter. The combination of assigning consequences rather than punishments and empathy can result in learning and hope. That is, if the employee knows someone else is sharing her emotions and fears, she no longer feels alone. This has a calming effect on the limbic region in her brain, allowing her to reflect on and learn from the consequences of her actions.

Pitfall #3: Everyone Is Not Equal

Empathy-based management maintains that every employee in the organization is accepted for who he is; understood as a person, having both thoughts and emotions, which include unique perspectives; and valued as both a person and an employee who makes valuable contributions to the organization.

But the practice of empathy-based management does not imply that every employee in your organization is equal. The reality is that there are significant differences among employees in terms of intelligence, ability, competence, work speed, personality, and motivation. These differences result in significant variances both in productivity and leadership ability among any organization's workers.

In each employee's best interest—in terms of perceived fairness or equity theory—as well as the organization's best interest, not everyone should be treated equally. Employees should be compensated based on performance and productivity. Those who are the most productive should be compensated accordingly. Those who have the most leadership ability are the ones who need to be promoted into management positions. (With one exception: any employee who has no desire to learn to be empathetic should never be promoted into a supervisor position.)

Baldoni supports the concept of unequal treatment of employees: "The most successful managers are those who devote a majority of their time to the high performers in their department. Managers must treat all of their employees fairly and equitably, but devoting time and resources to the high-potential people is wise."[30] Baldoni is suggesting that a part of empathy is understanding each employee as a unique person with differing aptitudes, work ethics, and attitudes. Make use of this understanding and devote your company's resources to those people who will bring the highest return for your investment.

In terms of empathy-based management, this is also critical for helping each employee in the organization grow personally and professionally because of the idea of equity—people in your organization will be treated fairly; they will be compensated for their professional growth and development

Pitfall #4: Failure to Hold Each Employee Accountable

Practicing empathy does not mean that you'll go easy on your employees. Rather, the empathetic manager holds the employee accountable for her actions. This is the only way the employee will learn. By not holding your workers accountable for their actions, you are enabling the employee's unhealthy behavior. Worse yet, if you "turn a blind eye" to the employee's misbehavior, you are robbing this person of learning from the consequences of her actions. The presence of an empathetic manager combined with experiencing the consequences of one's misconduct will aid in the learning process.

Pitfall #5: Managing Manipulative Employees

Being empathetic does not mean the manager allows the employee—and every organization has a few needy and manipulative employees—to manipulate her. For example, just because an employee is facing financial difficulties, the manager is not required to give her anything or do anything outside of company business and benefits. The empathetic manager is not required to give the employee a personal loan, babysit her children, or become her means of transportation. As a manager, you may do any of these activities if you want to be helpful (but then only occasionally), but the moment you sense that you are being manipulated, stop enabling your employee immediately.

Enabling is not in the employee's, the manager's, or the organization's best interest. Enabling teaches the employee to use the logical and creative abilities of his brain to exploit other people rather than to problem solve.

A healthy, beneficial empathetic response to a manipulative employee is: "Wow, that's terrible. What are *you* going to do about it?" This keeps the problem squarely where it belongs, as the employee's responsibility, rather than allowing it to become the manager's problem. Also it allows the manager to clearly set boundaries. On my office door, for example, I have a sign that reads, "DO NOT MISTAKE KINDNESS FOR WEAKNESS."

Creating an emotionally safe work environment requires managers to demonstrate not only empathy, understanding, and support but also to put boundaries around manipulative individuals. An empathetic manager therefore needs to watch the abusive employee closely, for the person bold enough to try to exploit his manager will also try to manipulate the most emotionally vulnerable employees in the organization. It is part of the manager's job, and good organizational policy, to protect such individuals from being taken advantage of by the impositions of another employee.

How do you set boundaries effectively around a manipulative employee? First, use as few words as possible when speaking to such a worker because anything you tell the manipulative employee may/will come back to haunt you. The exploitive employee will use your own words against you in order to gain an advantage whenever possible.

To enforce the boundaries you set, never tell the employee what *not* to do. Rather, explain to him what you will do if a behavior occurs or does not occur. Have the employee then repeat back to you exactly what you will do if a behavior occurs or does not occur. Thereafter, from day to day, problems will flare up with this manipulative employee, but to regain control with him or any difficult employee, simply say, "What did I tell you I was going to do if this behavior occurred again?"

More importantly, effectively setting boundaries around a manipulative employee requires a team effort. If the manipulative employee is male, you need to find a seasoned older man to mentor him. (Conversely, pair a female with an older woman.) Also, pair up the troubled employee with a street-smart coworker who will not tolerate obvious manipulations as they work together.

Recalling our earlier example, if the employee legitimately needs transportation, the manager should call a department meeting and create a team effort to help her with rides until her car is repaired.

In this way, the manipulative employee sees the manager effectively communicating with the entire department regarding both getting the employee the help she needs and setting expectations for how the manipulator is to behave as well.

Pitfall #6: The Manager Attempts to Be a Counselor to Employees

If your employee is dealing with severe emotional or traumatic issues, such as going through a divorce or grieving the death of a family member, always be empathetic and supportive, but encourage the employee to find a professional counselor to help them cope with the circumstances.

As the employee works through the grieving process, be as supportive as possible. For example, offer your employee time off as needed, be sure to attend the funeral service, or perhaps give the employee your personal cell phone number and instruct him to call you anytime as he works through this difficult time period.

If required, encouraging your employee to get professional counseling is fair to the employee, yourself, and the company. As a manager, your job is to maximize the organization's productivity and innovation, not to counsel people. Counseling people with critical mental health and emotional needs requires the expertise and insight of a credentialed psychologist or therapist, if not a psychiatrist. Leave counseling to trained professionals, and use your energy to focus on creating an emotionally supportive environment that is conducive to personal and professional employee growth.

Pitfall #7: Promoting a Person Who Cannot Empathize into a Supervisor Position

Apart from people with particular mental health issues, including autism and schizophrenia, every person is capable of learning to become more empathetic. But some people have no desire to develop their capacity to become more empathetic.

Both through conversations with your employee and by observing professional growth or stagnation over time, you will be able to discern if the person desires to learn to be more empathetic and grow into a leadership role. Do not promote anyone to a supervisory position who has no desire to learn how to become more empathetic toward others. One unempathetic supervisor can do serious damage to the employees' morale.

The ability to relate and respond to the feelings of another person is a key indicator of an emotionally and mentally healthy individual. Bowlby puts it even more strongly: "The capacity to make intimate emotional bonds with other individuals is regarded as a principle feature of effective personality functioning and mental health."[31]

If a manager both refuses to empathize with one's subordinates or refuses training to become more empathetic, the organization needs to remove the supervisory aspects of his position, if not move the person to a different role altogether.

EMPATHIZE WITH YOURSELF: UNDERSTANDING YOUR OWN NEEDS

Empathy-based management as a theory offers you, the manager, as many benefits as it does your employees, particularly the removal of stress in the workplace. Yes, it's a big outlay of energy to carefully word conversations with emotionally charged workers, but with practice it comes naturally. That said, however, I want to caution you not to set too high a standard for yourself or put too much pressure on yourself to "perform empathetically" flawlessly from the get-go. Empathizing takes hours of time and practice to perfect.

So no matter how stressful or demanding the atmosphere is at work, do not spend all of your emotional energy there. Save some of your mental energy for your own family. When you return home after work, your family will need you to be present, able to give them your undivided attention. Save enough energy to be able to empathize with your spouse and children rather than being spent, exhausted, and mentally distracted. This will strengthen your relationship with your family and make everyone's life more enjoyable at both home and at work.

CONCLUSION
In this chapter I have given some tools in order for you to understand and display empathetic behavior. These tools include how to: (1) figure out your employee's emotional state; (2) display

empathetic behaviors; and (3) join your employee in his emotional state. In order to be perceived as empathetic and honor your employee's emotions, it is important to choose words and thoughts that convey empathy, and display body language that is warm and accepting and communicates unconditional positive regard for your employee.

In chapter 5, you'll learn how to put all of the tools of empathy together and see how empathy-based management works in the business environment.

5

THE PRACTICE OF EMPATHY-BASED MANAGEMENT

Seek first to understand and then to be understood.
—STEPHEN COVEY

I will forget what you told me,
but I will never forget the way you made me feel.
—ANONYMOUS

The purpose of chapter 5 is to present an overview of how empathy-based management works in an organizational environment. As you likely recall from chapter 3, the three goals of empathy-based management are to create an emotionally secure work environment, give each employee hope, and help each employee grow personally and professionally. The entire organization benefits as each employee matures personally and professionally.

From chapter 4, we learned that there are two steps involved in the model of empathy-based management. The first step is to ask appropriate questions and then listen in order to understand the emotional state of each employee. The second step involves the manager's verbal and nonverbal response to each employee's emotional state. If everything is going well for your employee, give her a simple empathetic statement to communicate that you understand

and support her. For the majority of your employees, this will be the case most days. In this case, empathy-based management is very easy and effective to conduct. Empathetic communication with each employee will take only a few moments of your time at the start of each workday.

On the other hand, if something happened to the employee, she will tell an empathetic manager what happened. If the employee becomes emotional as she explains what happened, turn the worker's reaction into an intersubjective experience with the employee; go through the five steps of the intersubjective experience (presented in chapter 3) with your employee. If your employee is not emotional while explaining a difficulty that has occurred, use the empathetic choices model (presented in this chapter) in order to guide your employee to make the correct decision or display appropriate behavior.

Beyond the two-step model, there are issues that are integral parts of empathy-based management. The first issue is when a problem arises between the manager and an employee that requires the empathetic manager to repair any breaks in the relationship with the employee. The second issue is when the manager must handle employee misconduct in an empathetic manner.

A MODEL OF EMPATHETIC MANAGEMENT

Before Arriving at Work

Empathy-based management starts every morning when you wake up and get out of bed. Every morning do a mental self-check of your physical and mental well-being. Are you tired or well rested? Does a body part hurt, or are you ready for a full day of work? Are you in a good mood or angry or sad? This self-assessment or self-inventory is what psychologists describe as mindfulness.

Doing a mindfulness self-assessment before going to work every day is vital to being empathetic in your behavior at work. Understanding and being honest with yourself is very important every day. If you are in a bad mood, can you change your mood and act with empathy around your employees? Do you have the mental energy to deal with employee problems? Or, should you keep contact with employees (and everyone else) to a minimum today? It is vital that you are honest with yourself.

Starting Your Day at Work

If you are not in a mood to deal with other people when you arrive at work, it is important that you politely communicate with your employees that you have their best interests in mind, but today is not a good day for you to deal with employee issues. If you are honest with your employees, they will respect your authenticity. After lunch do another mindfulness exercise in order to evaluate if you are ready to interact with employees in the afternoon.

Let us assume you are now ready to respond to employee issues in an empathetic manner. The everyday model of empathy-based management is a two-part plan designed to handle many different scenarios.

Step #1: Greetings and Listening

Assuming you are in a mood to interact with each employee, have a brief but important interaction every morning as each employee arrives at work. Acknowledge each employee with a greeting and a question. For example, say, "Good morning. How are things going?" or "What's the forecast for your work today?" There is no one correct way to display empathetic behavior; rather, how you manifest empathy (both verbally and nonverbally) in a way that expresses respect and acceptance of the other person will depend on your personality. Thus, there are as many ways to make a personal connection with people as there are personalities. The key to the first step is for you to actively listen to your employee's response to the question.

In order to actively listen, give each employee your undivided attention. You must be both cognitively and emotionally present with each employee as they respond. Be aware of both your own body language and also the body language of the employee during the entire conversation. Are you displaying curiosity, acceptance, and encouragement? What is the nonverbal message each employee is trying to communicate to you? In other words, there is no "only going through the motions" while actively listening to an employee. This exercise each morning is vital because it sets the tone or adjusts each employee's emotional state at the beginning of each workday.

If you want your employee to share openly and honestly with you, first assure your employee each morning that you are there to listen without judgment and accept whatever the employee has to say, even though you may not agree with what is about to be said and no matter how personal it may be.

Baldoni explains the importance of your authenticity in every interaction with each employee:

> So, just what is communication? It is a process by which two or more people connect on a level that binds them together. Connection is a root of leadership; it is founded on authenticity, the soul of who you are as a leader. Your authenticity is your character, which is made up of your beliefs and values along with your commitment to your organization. Authenticity is readily apparent to those who work with you; it is how they picture you . . . For a leader, then, communication is the act of making authenticity transparent . . . When communications are clear and honest, motivation can occur.[32]

On a related issue, always be aware of what you observe but do not hear. Often what a person does not mention is just as important as what is articulated. If your employee's words and body language do not match, trust your employee's body language. For example, if your employee says everything is fine but her body is stiff and she will not make eye contact with you, you should believe her body language rather than her words.

Every morning when you have a brief visit with your employees, each employee will have one of three different responses: (1) everything is OK with the employee; (2) your employee shares an experience and becomes emotional when explaining what happened; or (3) your employee shares an experience and is not emotional. As we will see, each of these employee responses will require a different empathetic answer or reaction from you.

Let's now examine these three scenarios in more detail.

Step #2A: Everything Is OK with Employee

If in response to your question, your employee expresses that everything is OK, respond with an empathetic statement, such as, "Keep up the good work" or give the employee honest but encouraging feedback. Regarding an empathetic response, it is not what you say; it is your tone of voice. This applies to everything you say in life. Whether sincere, sarcastic, or negative, your employee will immediately focus on your tone of voice. A manager's tone of voice reveals her attitude toward the employee or situation; her intentions; whether or not she respects the employee; and her state of mind.

In giving an empathetic response, a little humor or a witty statement (not sarcastic) may help send your employee on her way with a smile. Finally, it is imperative that you always respect your employees' confidentiality and maintain your integrity by doing exactly what you say you're going to do.

Keep in mind as you interact with your employees at the start of each day that the more control you give your employees regarding their work, the more control you will gain. The more respect, control, and understanding you give away, the more your employees will give back to you. When an employee respects her manager, often she will deepen her own effort and resolve as she seeks to be respected by her manager.

Step #2B: Employee Shares an Experience, with Emotions

If your employee shares something that happened, and doing so evokes an emotional response in your employee, you must respond with empathy. More precisely, you should create an *intersubjective experience* with your employee (as presented in chapter 3) in order to calm down the limbic region and stop the releasing of stress hormones in your employee's brain. Once the emotional response in the employee's brain is calmed, then your employee can use the cognitive portion of his brain to begin to understand and work toward figuring out a solution to the event that occurred. As the personal crisis is resolved, your employee can then remain in a cognitive mode of thinking rather than an emotional mode throughout the rest of the workday.

Whenever any employee has an emotional response to any event, it is critical that you do not try to deny your employee his feelings. Instead, respond with empathy.

Step #2C: Employee Shares an Experience, without an Emotional Response

On the flip side, if your employee shares an important issue or a problem but the problem does not trigger an emotional response, then guide your employee through the empathetic choices model. (The empathetic choices model is a modified "love and logic" model, developed by Jim Fay, Foster Cline, and Charles Fay at The Love and Logic Institute, Inc.) Because the cognitive portion of your employee's brain is still functioning normally and is not being impaired by an emotional response, he can use logic to problem solve, and thus the empathetic choices model works well for problem solving. In the empathetic choices model, the manager helps the employee explore alternatives and allows the employee to make his own choice.

EMPATHETIC CHOICES MODEL

There are either three or five steps to the empathetic choices model, depending on the decision-making ability of each employee:

Step 1: Offer an empathetic response to the employee's problem, for example: "That is horrible."

Step 2: Ask how the employee plans to respond, for example: "What are you going to do to solve your problem?"

Step 3A: If the employee's solution sounds reasonable, affirm the employee's choice with empathy, for example: "Sounds like you have things figured out; go for it!"

Use step 3B if the employee's solution is unacceptable, unrealistic, or will not work.

Step 3B: Offer the employee several acceptable choices, beginning with, for example, the question, "Would you like to hear what I might suggest?"

Step 4: Make sure the employee understands the consequences of each choice by asking, for example: "So what might happen if you decide to—?"

Step 5: Give the employee permission to make a decision, and live with the consequences, for example: "Sounds good, let me know how things go for you."

The empathetic choices model allows your employee the opportunity to solve his problem in a safe environment. Many times an employee is not looking for advice when he shares a problem or issue; he just wants to talk to someone. In this case, steps 1 through 3A work well for empathetic listening without giving advice.

Alternatively, many times an employee will approach the manager with a problem, and she is looking for either help or for the manager to help solve her problem. A manager should never solve an employee's problem. This teaches the employee that she is not capable of solving her own problems. Rather, the empathetic choices model keeps the employee responsible for solving her own problems. Two important outcomes of the empathetic choices model are that your employee learns that she is capable of problem solving in her profession and, as your employee is responsible for solving her own problems, your workload will be reduced.

A SNAPSHOT OF EMPATHY-
BASED MANAGEMENT IN PRACTICE

In summary, in this basic model, every morning ask each employee how things are going. If everything is fine, send employees on their way with your blessing. If there is a problem and an employee is emotional, take her through an intersubjective experience in order to create understanding, calm the brain's emotional response, and find a solution. If there is a problem and she does not have an emotional response, guide her through the empathetic choices model in order to problem solve. Finally, always end your interactions with each employee with a word of support, hope, or encouragement.

We are now going to turn to two important issues any manager must face: (1) problems between you and your employee, and (2) dealing with employee discipline.

ISSUE #1: PROBLEM BETWEEN MANAGER AND EMPLOYEE

Theodore Roosevelt once stated, "No one cares how much you know, until they know how much you care." This is especially true regarding the employee-manager relationship.

If a problem or personal issue should arise between you and an employee, it is your responsibility to repair the relationship. The manager needs to initiate repair of the relationship and utilize the intersubjective experience model as a framework to help repair the relationship. Recall from chapter 3 and step 2B in this chapter, the five steps of the intersubjective experience.

But in Step 5, as you clarify the employee's point of view non-defensively and with empathy, also clarify your motives for your actions involved in the problem with your employee. Allow your employee to respond with questions or further rebuttal from his perspective. You and your employee will give and take until you reach a mutual understanding of what happened and why. Together, you will cocreate meaning to the event.

Because the relationship between the manager and the employee is a superior/subordinate relationship, any attempts to resolve the problem in the relationship must be conducted in a perceived fair manner. If the issue is serious or personal, you may decide to bring in another person to act as an arbitrator during the meeting in the interest of perceived fairness and objectivity. The arbitrator may be another manager or employee in the organization whom everyone respects and knows to be impartial.

It is critical to address any rift between the manager and the employee in a perceived fair manner, because once the subordinate perceives he has no control over his work life, then energy, effort, and motivation all dramatically fall as the limbic region releases stress hormones into the employee's brain resulting from the negative reaction. An employee who feels he has no control in his work life will focus on being angry at his manager rather than focusing on work, and his coworkers may also be influenced by his emotional negativity. By contrast, the employee who feels he has some control in his work life will spend little energy trying to undermine his manager's authority.

PASSING ON YOUR VALUES TO YOUR EMPLOYEES

Values are passed from manager to employees in two ways: by what employees see and what they experience while interacting with their supervisor. Whatever values one's supervisor's behavior displays will be the values learned by each employee and will become the values of your workforce.

An Example of a Manager Resolving a Dispute with an Employee

In this example, John is irritated with his manager, Jesse, because he feels that he has been unfairly passed over for a promotion.

John (employee): Can I have a minute of your time?

Jesse: Sure, pull up a chair. How may I help you?

John: It's not fair. Jose got promoted to be our supervisor, and I didn't. I have been working my ass off, and you know it. I am a harder worker than Jose, and I am tired of getting passed over.

Jesse: Wow. I had no idea this was an issue. Thank you for telling me about this. I can understand why you are angry. To be unfairly overlooked is a horrible experience.

John: Yes, it sucks, and it is not fair. But . . . *you* made the final decision on who got promoted.

Jesse: So, are you angry at me for this overlooked promotion?

John: No, no, I am not mad at you. Um . . . I am just very irritated that once again I got passed over.

Jesse: Actually, you have a right to be angry with me if you felt my judgment was unfair. But thank you for trusting me enough to come talk to me about this issue. I recognize, and I think almost everyone around here recognizes, that you are one of the hardest workers in our company. When it is crunch time, you, more than any other person in your department, help keep us on schedule. I don't want to lose you. I know you could have just quit over this issue. John, thank you for coming and talking with me about this issue rather than just quitting.

John: You are welcome. But you just admitted that I am one of your best workers. So, why did Jose get promoted and not me?

Jesse: That is a fair question to ask. Over a year ago, Jose came into my office and expressed an interest in a supervisor position. I told him I would make no guarantees, but I asked him if he would be willing to start training to someday become a supervisor. I told him that his ability to become a supervisor would depend on his performance, his ability to problem solve, and his ability to lead his team to meet the goals that we laid out. He has worked very hard over the past year, and he has been given the opportunity. Now we will see how well he performs. As a supervisor, Jose has my full support, and as a worker you have my full support.

John: Well, what about me? You just admitted that I have your full support. When are you going to make me a supervisor?

Jesse: Actually, John, let me restate what I think you are saying. I don't make anyone a supervisor. What I think you are saying is that you understand that your ability to become a supervisor will depend on your performance and ability. This is why training is required. You are asking for the opportunity to start training in order to someday be given a trial position so that you can demonstrate your ability to manage. If successful, your role as supervisor would become a permanent position. Is this what you are asking?

John: Yes, that is what I have been trying to say. So, are you going to let me start training?

Jesse: Before I say yes, I need some clarification. I call this my miracle question. If in six months, you could have any job in this company, what would it be? What is your dream job?

John: I want be the CEO of our company!

Jesse: Actually, realistically, twenty years from now, I could see you as our CEO. It will take at least five promotions, and each promotion will depend on your performance at the new position.

John: Oh, well . . .

Jesse: Are there any jobs that you would like to move into right now?

John: This may sound weird, but one job that I would like to move into is sales. I could make a lot more money than I am making right now. My fiancée and I could really use the extra money.

Jesse: As hard as you work, you might do very well in sales. Let me ask you another question. Which would you prefer: to start training to move into sales or to start training to become a supervisor?

John: I would definitely prefer to get into sales.

Jesse: Would you like me to transfer you to our marketing department? Your job over there would be probationary and depend on your performance. With your work ethic, you will do well. But on a personal note, I hate to see you leave this department. I enjoy working with you. But I also know that you will probably make a lot more money for both yourself and for our company in a sales position. So would you like me to recommend a transfer?

John: Definitely. Thank you.

In this example, John is very irritated at Jesse for his perceived injustice. Jesse does not deny his perception; he validates his reaction with empathy. After mutually sharing each person's interpretation of the event in an emotionally safe environment created by Jesse's ability to empathize, the limbic region in John's brain calms down. Once the emotions in John's brain calm down in response to Jesse's empathy, together they cocreate new meaning to the event. John is upset because he believes he has the ability to become a manager, and he was unfairly overlooked. John is also upset because he is getting married soon, and he needs to earn more money. Jesse responds with empathy and empowers him by giving him the opportunity to make more money at his job. This new opportunity not only empowers John, it also gives him hope and is the source of motivation to create a better life for both him and his new family.

ISSUE #2: CONSEQUENCES WHEN AN EMPLOYEE BREAKS COMPANY POLICY

It is not a pleasant task to confront an employee who breaks company policy. Confronting the employee with empathy-based management, instead of traditional management practices, works in the best interest of both the employee and the organization. This may sound like a conflict of interest, but in reality, it is the best way to manage employee behavior and help people to learn and grow. Also differing from traditional management, empathy-based management does not punish employees; rather, employees learn from the consequences of their misconduct.

Punishment is determined by an authority figure, or in this case, you, the manager. By contrast, consequences are the natural result of one's actions. For example, the consequence of staying up too late at night results in you feeling overly tired and having difficulty concentrating the next morning. In the case of empathy-based management, consequences come from your organization's rules, rather than from your discretion. Punishment is often associated with irritation or anger on behalf of the manager. Consequences, however, allow you to be empathetic toward the difficulties your employee may be experiencing as a result of misconduct.

HELP YOUR EMPLOYEES LEARN FROM THE CONSEQUENCES OF THEIR ACTIONS

You can use empathy to help employees learn from the consequences of their behavior. The process for doing so has four steps. This entire approach is relatively straightforward and is an effective way to help each employee accept and learn from the consequences of his mistake(s).

Lay Out Expectations as People Are Hired

Regarding consequences for misconduct, empathy-based management begins at the point of hire, when each new employee receives a handbook. The handbook contains all of the company's policies and explicitly outlines expectations for employee conduct. It also clearly defines the consequences for each category of misbehavior by the employee. For example, for one type of misconduct, the first offense will result in a warning; for another type of behavior, the employee will receive a one-day suspension; for other categories of offenses, the employee will be terminated; etc. The employee handbook not only contains consequences for misbehavior, it also clearly outlines both the values of the organization and expected behaviors.

It is not unreasonable for your organization to expect every employee to be dedicated and ethical, competent, and an enjoyable coworker. Most new hires will not have all qualities, but as an empathetic manager, it is your job to develop these qualities in each employee. And in an empathetic work environment, these behaviors have an opportunity to occur.

As part of the hiring process, each new hire is required to read the employee handbook. Once the employee reads the handbook, the manager answers any questions, and the new hire signs, as part of her contract, that she understands and agrees to abide by all company policies set forth in the handbook.

An Empathetic Model of Learning through Consequences

When an employee breaks a company policy, she must always be required to face the consequences of her action. Being empathetic on your behalf does not mean intentionally overlooking her misconduct. To the contrary, to have empathy means you understand and are working for both the organization's and the employee's best interests. To ignore misconduct would be in neither party's best interest. It would not be in the interest of the organization, because the employee would be allowed to misuse organizational resources and/or disrupt the work environment. And it would not be in the best interest of the employee, because you would be robbing your employee of an opportunity to learn, grow, and become more ethical.

Whenever an employee breaks a company policy, your response should guide your employee's behavior through a four-step reaction that reflects empathy on behalf of management.

Step 1: Respond with Empathy

When an employee breaks company policy, *always*, your first words need to be an empathetic response. For example: "Oh, no"; "Uh, oh"; "This is painful"; "Ouch"; "Oh Crap"; or "Momma-Mia."

The key to your initial response is not the exact words you use, rather your tone of voice. Your nonverbal reaction must match the emotional state of your employee, be it embarrassment, fear, shame, or anger. But do not reflect the employee's negative emotional state with negativity; rather, as an empathetic manager, reflect the employee's dismay with understanding and empathy. For example, you might say, "This is so sad" or "This is tragic."

Whenever responding to an employee in a disciplinary setting, please keep in mind to not use sarcasm. Only display sincere empathy toward the employee and his present predicament. Also, never get angry at the employee. Instead, only empathize with the employee's distress. And finally, never yell at the employee. Instead, always use a calm but firm and reassuring voice when addressing employee misconduct.

Step 2: Investigate the Consequences of the Employee's Action

Review the employee handbook with your employee to find the consequences of the misconduct. With great empathy, you are required to enforce company policy. Your employee is required to live up to the agreement of consequences set forth in the employee handbook. During step 2, the tone of your voice must be calm, gentle, and compassionate, but also firm and professional.

Learning the consequences of the misconduct may trigger an emotional response in your employee's brain. She may display a variety of different emotions, including embarrassment, anger, or sadness. She may become very emotional or may become withdrawn and act like she'd like to hide from your presence. Or else, she may try to argue in order to try to get you to not enforce the consequences of the misconduct. You must remain firm in the enforcement of the consequences.

Step 3: Help Your Employee to Emotionally Calm Down

After learning of the consequences of the misconduct, the amygdala in the employee's brain is most likely triggered. Now, it's time to help your employee calm down by empathizing with his emotional state.

During this step, it is very important for you to separate the person from the behavior. Always affirm your employee as a person, but stand firm on the consequences of the misconduct. For example, you must be sincere, but perhaps say something to the effect of: "Wow, I really was not expecting this. What an unfortunate thing to do. Actually, I am surprised because you are one of my best employees."

If your employee needs more emotional support, guide him through the five steps of the intersubjective experience discussed previously. As the manager, you need to be able to empathize with and understand your employee's feelings. Your employee's emotional state will respond to your emotional reaction and your ability to empathize. Using the five steps of the intersubjective experience, your employee's emotions will begin to calm down as he experiences your support and unconditional positive regard toward him, in spite of the misconduct.

Through this entire process, make no remarks that discount the feelings of the employee. For example, never say something to the effect of, "Don't worry about it" or "No big deal." If your employee is having an emotional reaction to the consequences of her misconduct, it is a big deal to her. Instead, remain emotionally supportive through acknowledging her emotional state until the limbic region in her brain has time to calm down.

If your employee is very upset and wants to leave, allow her to leave. She needs time by herself in order to calm down. This is a good thing. The employee knows herself and might be afraid that she will say something to the manager that she will later regret. Therefore, in response to your employee's emotional duress, be empathetic and give her time to emotionally calm down.

Step 4: Give Your Employee Time,
and Allow Consequences to Do the Teaching

After your employee calms down, he will need time to start using the cognitive portion of his brain to begin thinking rationally and start learning from the consequences of his actions. As a manager, do not try to teach him anything. Do not lecture him on the "consequences."

At this stage, for you to suggest anything would be counterproductive. Allow your employee to learn from the consequences of her behavior. Your employee is intelligent, and if given the opportunity, she will learn from her mistake. For you to explain what an adult should learn would insult her intelligence. Do, however, make yourself available to listen if the employee would like to discuss the matter in a rational manner.

Over time, your employee's values will develop from what she observes occurring within the organization, including your values as manager. Your employee will not be able to hear any lecture from you when the neocortex of her brain is shut down due to an emotional response during a time of interpersonal crises. Rather, any "lesson" from you will be met with anger and hostility.

Knowing this, let the consequences of her actions do the teaching, and instead be a source of support, understanding, and compassion. With consequences to one's misconduct, all of the learning is internalized, and the focus is on self and learning, rather than being angry with an external punishment.

An Example of Punishment Versus Consequences

In this example, the company's CEO wants to punish an employee. Jesse explains to the CEO why using consequences for one's actions is more effective than punishment.

> **CEO:** You are being too easy on your employee. He messed up. He needs to be punished. I don't care about the employee's feelings, I care about results.

Jesse: Are you suggesting that my empathy for our employee's embarrassment and guilt right now means that there should be no consequences for his misconduct?

CEO: It sure seems like that is what you are saying.

Jesse: By understanding his embarrassment with him, I am trying to help him avoid feeling shamed around his coworkers. I am trying to help him not make an additional mistake like quit his job or lash out at management.

CEO: OK, I see your point. But he still needs to be punished so he understands what he did is wrong. And it will make him an example for the other employees.

Jesse: Trust me, he knows what he did was wrong. But I am concerned that he does not understand that you and I care about him as a person and not just as an employee. He may think that I only care about the rules. If so, he will feel isolated in his distress.

CEO: So, what are you suggesting we do?

Jesse: Our employee is required to face the consequences of his actions. He already knows that. But if I am empathetic toward his situation and the resulting consequences, he will learn more from the consequences of his actions. If no one empathizes with him, he will only feel embarrassment and anger. Also, by taking the time to care about his emotional distress, I am teaching him the importance of company policy and the value of both appropriate behavior within our organization and how much we value him as an employee.

This example lays out the essence of empathy-based management. Jesse cares about the employee and comprehends how he may be feeling emotionally as he is required to face the consequences of his actions. Jesse is not angry with the employee, rather, concerned that he learns from the consequences of his behavior in an emotionally safe environment so he has an opportunity to grow and mature as a result.

RESULTS OF PUNISHMENT VS. RESULTS OF CONSEQUENCES

At this point, it would be a useful exercise to compare the effects on an employee of punishment vs. consequences.

RESULTS OF PUNISHMENT

- The manager may be irritated or angry.
- The employee becomes irritated or angry at the manager.
- The employee's amygdala and limbic region in the brain is triggered.
- The employee's mental energy is focused on being angry at the manager.
- The employee cannot problem solve while the amygdala is triggered and filling the brain with stress hormones that inhibit thinking.
- The employee does not learn from the mistake and has an opportunity to blame the manager.
- The manager is the judge.
- The manager utilizes her power.
- The employee may feel powerless and possibly a sense of servitude to the manager.
- The employee may enter a deep sense of shame.
- The employee may become disenfranchised from both the manager and the organization.
- The employee may lose hope. The loss of hope kills employee motivation.

RESULTS OF CONSEQUENCES

- The manager is empathetic, understanding, and compassionate.
- The manager expresses unconditional positive regard for the employee as a person.

- The employee is not angry at the manager.
- The employee appreciates the manager's understanding and support.
- The employee's brain releases oxytocin, which calms the limbic region.
- The limbic region in the employee's brain calms down.
- The employee starts using the cognitive portion of the brain to problem solve.
- The employee's focus is on his own behavior, and he learns from the consequences of his actions.
- The manager is allowed to feel sad for the employee.
- The manager is perceived to be a "supportive" leader rather than the source of the employee's problems.
- The employee can take ownership of the problem in a safe environment.
- The employee is allowed to hurt from the inside.
- The employee feels safe and can be honest and vulnerable.
- The employee is his own judge.
- The employee retains her sense of dignity and self-efficacy.
- The employee is not disenfranchised; rather, loyalty to both the manager and the organization may grow as she feels supported during this time of duress.
- The employee is given hope and retains his motivation toward his career.

PRACTICING PATIENCE

The way the human brain is strengthened is similar to the muscles in your body. Like a muscle, if exercised, any part of the human brain will grow stronger through neuroplasticity. For example, after practicing the piano or giving a sales presentation or doing bookkeeping, give your brain time to rest, and the responsible area of your brain will grow stronger and become better at the activity. Likewise, the more the employee practices an activity, the stronger her brain grows and the more skilled she becomes at conducting a particular activity.

Scientists refer to neuroplasticity as a characteristic of the brain to change and grow in response to events and activities in our lives. *Neuro* refers to nerves in the brain, and *plasticity* refers to being moldable. Thus the human brain can mold itself to learn and master almost any new skill. Neuroplasticity refers to changes in neuropathways resulting from new tasks, changes in the external environment, or from bodily injury.

I am reminded of neuroplasticity every four years when I watch the Olympics. A human being can choose any Olympic sport. With enough practice at the chosen sport, it is possible for the dedicated athlete to improve enough over time to make it to the Olympics. This shows how neuroplasticity within the human brain working in coordination with the body is a truly remarkable feature.

Within an emotionally secure work environment, where employees' brains are able to focus on problem solving because of a stable emotional environment, managers need to give employees time in order to think and problem solve. If given time, mastery of a new skill will result as the human brain learns and grows. This principle has a variety of applications within the workplace. For example, when an employee is required to face the consequences of an action, once the limbic region calms down, the employee will need time to process and learn from the mistake. In time the employee's brain will learn and grow from the experience.

Another example of giving employees adequate time to think would be before a large meeting where an important decision needs to be made. At least twenty-four hours before the meeting time, the manager should pull all key people who are making the decision aside and fully brief them on the decision to be made at the meeting. The manager needs to give each participant all the materials related to the decision, go over all of the issues, and answer any questions. After each participant is fully informed, their brains have twenty-four hours to process the information, problem solve, and develop pertinent questions. The opinions the participants bring into the meeting will be significantly more insightful than if the meeting is the first time the committee members see the relevant materials required to make an informed decision.

Finally, and perhaps most importantly regarding being empathetic, if you are in a private meeting with an employee discussing a problem and you don't know what to do, stop and give your brain time to think. If you are unsure of what is the best course of action, tell your employee that you need to do some research or talk to other involved parties, and you can reconvene later, perhaps the following day. This will give your brain time to think through the situation and come up with a reasonable plan of action. With empathy-based management, whenever you are in doubt of the correct response, take time out and give your brain time to process in order to proceed with the best course of action.

GIVING YOUR BRAIN TIME TO THINK

When an employee comes into your office and is very emotional about an issue or mad at you, it is important to not respond immediately. Through empathy toward other people's emotional states, the human brain is wired to respond to anger with alarm, most often as fight or flight, which is usually expressed as anger, rather than with logic and reasoning. It is very important to give your brain a few moments to calm down in order to respond with understanding and empathy rather than anger. Your employee may be looking for a fight, and if you respond with anger, you will be sucked into an unwinnable battle. (You may win the argument, but you will have lost your employee's confidence and loyalty.) Instead, give your brain time to calm down so you can respond with empathy.

Responding with empathy is the only way you will be able to not give into your employee's demands and keep your employee's trust by disarming your employee's anger.

When you need to give both your brain and your employee's brain time to calm down and think, promise to answer your employee's question or address his concern. But also ask permission to delay your answer and explain that his perception is more important than yours, and you desire to respond appropriately. For example, say, "I am learning a lot of new information from our conversation. You have just brought up some very important information; I want to make sure that I fully understand everything that you are saying before I respond. Is this OK?"

The reason your employee's perception or opinion is more important than the manager's is because you cannot help your employee until you understand his interpretation of the event. Also, as long as your employee is in fight-or-flight mode, your opinion does not matter. What is more important is that you understand your employee's perception so that you can calm down the anger in the affective portion of your employee's brain through empathizing with your employee's interpretation of the event and displaying to your employee understanding and unconditional positive regard.

DEALING WITH EMPLOYEE ANGER

Of all the intense emotional states the employee may display, anger, especially if directed toward you, may be the most difficult for you to not take personally and to respond appropriately to. The human brain is wired to respond to anger with either fear or anger. In the case of anger, since the human brain naturally reads the emotional states of other people, the intensity of emotion created in the limbic region in your employee's brain will trigger the amygdala in your own brain to release stress hormones and shut down the cognitive portion of your brain. Thus the neocortex of both brains will be shut down as you and your employee enter into a fight-or-flight mode in response to each other's emotional states.

Sensing your employee's anger, you may be tempted to respond to anger with anger. Instead of responding in anger, as a manager you need to respond with empathy. Empathy, understanding, and responding with unconditional positive regard create a sense of connection. From this sense of connection, oxytocin is released in the brain and turns off the fight-or-flight response. Your employee's amygdala stops the flood of stress hormones into the human brain. Thus, the limbic region in your employee's brain starts to calm down.

An appropriate response by the manager might be: "I sense that you are very angry with me, and probably for a good reason. You are an excellent employee and person whom I deeply respect. I value you and your thoughts. So your anger toward me is very important to me. But first I need to make sure that you and I are not miscommunicating. Let us backtrack for a minute. I want to make sure I understand exactly what just happened."

Again, as manager, you must focus on your employee's interpretation of the event, rather than the actual event itself. Then, proceed to steps 1 through 5 of the intersubjective experience. The key to handling the employee's anger is to demonstrate to the employee, through both words and body language, that anger like any other emotion does not result in your rejection. Instead, he is held in high regard, and there must be an important reason for him to be angry. Like any emotion, an empathetic manager is not threatened by anger; rather, you are able to understand the reasons for and co-regulate your employee's anger.

Your employee learns that you are an emotionally safe person to confide in and that the organization is an emotionally safe place to work. He learns that even anger is met with a safe response, and being emotionally upset does not threaten his own self-preservation, including job security if he displays anger. He learns that anger is not an emotion that is required to be buried or controlled at all costs, nor is it a source of shame. And he learns that differences of opinion are not only accepted, they are valued by the organization.

It becomes very difficult to continually innovate and move an organization forward if no one questions the wisdom of management. (Wisdom is simply the correct application of knowledge, and there are occasionally unforeseen applications that management overlooks during its consideration.) As each employee comes to understand that the organization is an emotionally safe work environment, the limbic region in each employee's brain stabilizes over time as the prefrontal neocortex begins to build bridges and starts regulating the amygdala. In other words, the rational neocortex of each employee's brain begins to influence and control emotions created by the amygdala. Over time, there is less reason for the employee to become angry when he feels accepted and understood. With stable emotions, both you and your employees can use your mental energy to focus on innovative ideas that will move your company forward.

If, however, you react to your employee's anger with anger, he will continue to struggle with his anger. He will not learn how to self-regulate his emotions, including anger. And your relationship with your employee will continue to be stressed, rather than supportive and conducive to professional growth.

CONCLUSION

In this chapter we laid out a basic model of empathy-based management. Remember that employees will change their behavior in response to their supervisor changing her style of management.

When you as the manager start developing a personal relationship with each employee, your employees will have no choice but to change their attitudes and behavior. Every morning you make a personal connection with each employee, you allow them to experience your support as they begin their workday. Throughout each day every employee knows that you are a dependable resource should any problems arise.

CONCLUSION: AN INVITATION FROM THE AUTHOR

Action follows hope.
—ANONYMOUS

One conversation can change a life forever.
—ANONYMOUS

I wrote this book to present a new style of management, one based on empathy. The underlying assumption of empathy-based management is that *connection* to other people—rather than *correction*—is required for professional growth and long-term motivation to occur. Based on this assumption, during every inter-action with each employee throughout each day, build upon your relationships and provide the emotional support required for each person to be engaged and successful at their jobs. Work hard to achieve the goal of having each employee:

- Be productive and enjoy their accomplishments;
- Grow both personally and professionally;
- Be successful on the job and in life;
- Be ethical as they begin to experience how their actions affects the lives of others; and

- Become motivated to achieve self-actualization or reach their potential in life.

As we have come to understand, having employees grow, mature, and reach their potential is in the best interest of the company. Competent, capable, ethical, and committed employees are the workers that will make any company successful. Helping each employee mature and become successful both professionally and personally is one of the best investments any company can make. And incorporating empathy into your management practices makes these goals possible. The appendixes and worksheets that follow this section will help you better understand and utilize empathy-based management in your organization.

I would like to take this opportunity to summarize, in a nutshell, why empathy-based management is important for employee motivation and success. If a manager speaks in a harsh or critical tone of voice, displays threatening body language, or attempts to use mind games in order to motivate an employee, the brain of the subordinate is designed to immediately focus on the supervisor's nonverbal behavior, rather than on the intended message.

Whenever a manager argues with an employee or exhibits any form of threatening behavior, as perceived by the employee, this will cause a chemical reaction in the brain of the employee. As the employee perceives the manager's behavior to be threatening, the brain's amygdala is triggered, causing the adrenal glands to release the stress hormones adrenaline and cortisol. This is known as the fight-or-flight response. These stress hormones will inhibit thinking from occurring in the cortex of the brain, and an emotional response will consume the brain as the stress hormones focus the human brain's attention on the threatening behavior, and any thinking that occurs will be about possible ways to avoid or escape the perceived threat.

After the emotional confrontation with the manager, the employee's brain will remain in fight-or-flight mode. With elevated levels of stress hormones in the bloodstream, he will spend the rest of the workday mentally dwelling on the event and the damaged relationship with the manager. If the employee feels misunderstood or the manager's behavior is perceived to be unfair, he will invest incredible amounts of emotional energy being angry with his supervisor. As the human brain is consumed by negative emotions, the employee is unable to focus on the work at hand.

From a neurobiological perspective, the reason you must be empathetic in your management practices is that the brain will trigger a different chemical reaction when the manager understands and empathizes with the employee's perspective and the worker feels unconditionally accepted and understood. As your employee understands that you care about her as a person and as a trustworthy friend, the pituitary gland within her brain releases oxytocin, which calms down the amygdala and in turn calms any negative emotions occurring within the limbic region of the brain. Oxytocin has the opposite effect of the fight-or-flight response. It calms down the limbic region and allows the employee to use the cortex of the brain for thinking and problem solving. Following this chemical reaction, the employee can spend her day focused on her job and the work at hand.

Equally important, over time, in an emotionally secure work environment, the prefrontal cortex of the human brain is able to regulate the limbic region so workers can remain calm and problem solve as issues occur. The opposite is true for the human brain of employees who work in an emotionally unstable environment. The amygdala is easily triggered, and stress hormones released by the limbic region will shut down thinking and problem solving as needed in order to survive perceived threatening behaviors by the manager. The human brain is wired first and foremost for survival. The human amygdala is continuously monitoring for possible threats, and reaction speed for the limbic region is significantly faster than the reaction speed of the neocortex of the brain. In a perceived hostile work environment, the cortex of the human brain is shut down by the limbic region before it has time to process possible perceived threats.

Thus, as a manager, it is your nonverbal message, rather than your spoken words, that will have a greater impact on the long-term behavior of your employees. For personal and professional growth to occur, connection to a mentor rather than correction is required for the correct wiring of the human brain. This is the essence of why empathy-based management is crucial for long-term employee growth and motivation.

As I write this conclusion, I am watching my eight-year-old son practice basketball with his teammates. I can't help but wonder who he will be working for in another decade at his first part-time job. More importantly, I wonder how his boss will treat him or if his manager will view him as just another productive input.

With these questions in mind, I am concerned with the direction that corporate America is headed. I am convinced that empathy-based management is a healthier and more effective way to manage your employees than traditional management practices based on temporary inducements. The practice of empathy-based management needs to become a conversation in your organization and across corporate America about what works and what is ineffective in the real world. I hope you'll make this book a starting point for this much-needed discussion.

I would like you to do two things. First, put into practice in your organization the principles and techniques explained in this book. Second, please have an honest and frank conversation with me. I am very interested in hearing what works and what does not work. I would appreciate hearing how you are implementing empathy-based management in your organization's management philosophy and practices. Together, through our conversations, we can continue to build upon and refine the theory of empathy-based management to the benefit of every person in your organization and the organization itself. This is an open invitation to continue this conversation regarding how to incorporate empathy into your management practices.

You can contact me at:
George Langelett
Box 504, Scobey Hall 110
South Dakota State University
Brookings, SD 57007
Or by email: georgelangelett@outlook.com

Thank you. I look forward to hearing from you.

ACKNOWLEDGMENTS

I am humbled by the realization that this book wouldn't be a reality if it were not for the empathy of many people who understood my desires and, in response, helped make it possible for me to write it.

First, I need to thank my loving wife, Lara, who was willing to work double time so that I could write this book.

I wish to personally thank my parents, Evert and Betty, who have always supported me in anything I have chosen to do. Next, I wish to personally thank Dr. Laurie Nichols and Dr. Barry Dunn for the opportunity to write this book. Also I thank President David Chicoine, Dr. Eluned Jones, Dr. Dennis Papini, and Julia Karlstad for their continual support and encouragement. Thank you Kuo-Liang (Matt) Chang, Renae Kuhl, and Zhiguang (Gerald) Wang for taking time to read my drafts and provide useful feedback.

I thank Jesus Christ for being my empathetic role model. And I need to thank Mr. Larry Euhle, Mr. James Hanna, Mr. Charles Kuivinen, Mr. Craig Peters, Dr. Greg Wegner, and Dr. Kent Koppelman for being my mentors. Thank you Thomas Clark, Brent Larson, Tom, Howard and Vincent Holloway, Troy Alfson, and Mical Blue for your unwavering friendship and support.

I would like to thank Linda O'Doughda, my editor, whose countless hours of hard work and ability to separate wheat from chaff made this book possible; Jay Hodges, my finishing editor, whose elegance in word choice I will always admire; Pam Nordberg, for her diligent review of my manuscript; and Kim Lance, who designed a superb book cover; Bryan Carroll for his unwavering support; Corrin Foster for her ingenuity and all her hard work to market my book and make this project successful; and the rest of the team at Greenleaf Book Group, LLC, for their continual encouragement. I take sole responsibility for any mistakes or omissions found within this book.

Appendix A

A JOURNEY THROUGH MANAGEMENT THEORIES OF MOTIVATION

The history of management theory taught in academia is rich with innovative thinking and understanding regarding human motivation. Some theories have been disregarded over time, while others have proven to be leaps forward in our modeling of human motivation. The purpose of this appendix is to review several of the major theories of motivation in the management of employees. I will review seven of the dominant theories of employee motivation found within the management literature today. Each review is followed by a response from the perspective of empathy-based management.

THEORY #1: TAYLOR, THE FATHER OF SCIENTIFIC MANAGEMENT

Frederick Winslow Taylor (1856–1915) is known as the father of scientific management. With a background in mechanical engineering, Taylor applied an engineering approach to managing a company. He focused on industrial efficiency, and his work was later referred to as the field of time and motion. Taylor's management model was to view an organization as a machine—highly bureaucratic, with tight, centralized control. He viewed the physical movements of every worker as scientifically calculated to maximize production, to create a company run like a well-oiled machine.

Perspective from Empathy-Based Management

Frederick Taylor helped management theory become a formal field of study. Coming out of a mechanical engineering background, with a focus on process, his exclusive focus on the cognitive portion of the human brain set a precedent for subsequent research on human motivation. This was an unfortunate precedent to set because his exclusive focus on the cognitive side of the human brain set a precedent for management theory for the next century. In other words, Taylor modeled workers like any other productive input, rather than as persons whose actions are governed by both thoughts and feelings. By contrast, empathy-based management recognizes that to ignore human emotion is to deny one's humanity and violate one's sense of value and self-worth. The long-term productivity of any company is determined more by the attitudes of the workforce than by how efficiently the movement of each employee is calculated.

THEORY #2: MASLOW, FATHER OF THE HIERARCHAL APPROACH TO HUMAN NEEDS

In response to Taylor's engineering approach to management, Abraham Maslow (1908–1970) took a human relations approach to management and suggested that workers are human beings, each with needs that we are looking to satisfy. For Maslow, all human motivation is a process that starts with the identification of needs deficiency. Maslow grouped needs by level, from lowest to highest: (1) physiological needs, including food, shelter, and clothing; (2) safety and security; (3) need for love, relationships, and belongingness; (4) esteem and social status; (5) self-actualization, the need to reach one's potential. According to Maslow, not all needs are equal in their importance. Lower-level needs must be met first. Until a lower-level need is met, a person cannot advance and attempt to satisfy the next level of needs. For example, until a person has food, shelter, and clothing, he cannot go on to try to pursue his need for security or belongingness.

According to Maslow, needs identification is the source of motivation for employees at work. For example, at the most basic needs level, the employee needs to earn enough money to be able to afford food and housing; at the next level the employee needs security, namely job security, etc.

Perspective from Empathy-Based Management

Maslow's hierarchy of needs is a much more accurate appraisal of human behavior than Taylor's model, but it is an incomplete model. Human beings have needs, and the quest to satisfy one's needs does motivate people. But the highest level of need that people experience in life is not to achieve self-actualization. Rather, once an individual has achieved self-actualization, or reached his potential and then gone onto maturity, the highest human need is to help other people reach their own self-actualization. For the emotionally healthy adult who becomes successful, one of the most fulfilling things to do with the acquired success is to help others reach their own self-actualization. From the organizational perspective, the most satisfying thing a manager can do is to help employees reach their potential.

THEORY #3: SKINNER, FATHER OF BEHAVIOR MODIFICATION

Burrhus Frederic (B. F.) Skinner (1904–1990) was a professor of psychology at Harvard University. Skinner created an operant conditioning chamber. With the conditioning chamber, Skinner would place animals on a schedule of behavior modification through positive reinforcement, negative reinforcement, and punishment. For example, if a rat pushed one lever, it would receive a piece of food. If the rat pushed a different lever, nothing would result. Thus, Skinner could modify behavior over time through reinforcements. This is the idea of management through "sticks and carrots." A "carrot" refers to a reward placed in front of a mule to lead it in the right direction. A "stick" is a punishment used to spank the mule in order to alter the mule's behavior.

Skinner focused solely on observable behavior. He believed all behavior is learned, and through proper conditioning, the desired new behavior would result. Systematic behavior change is what Skinner called operant conditioning. (At the time of Skinner's work, functional magnetic resonance imaging, fMRI, had not yet been invented; therefore, it was impossible to analyze the workings of the human brain.) Skinner rejected the notion that thoughts and feelings drive human behavior; rather, he believed emotions were a condition that could be treated scientifically. Skinner's work deeply influenced the philosophy of management regarding employee motivation, and the management philosophy of many organizations today is still based on behaviorism techniques.

Perspective from Empathy-Based Management

Behaviorism and empathy-based management are diametrically opposed management theories for three reasons. First, behaviorism's utilization of rewards and punishment has a short-term focus. Skinner did not investigate long-term behavior consequences of behaviorism techniques. Second, Skinner felt the inner workings of the human brain were both impossible to accurately understand and irrelevant to human motivation. Behaviorism ignores both the limbic region and the neocortex (cognitive portion) of the human brain when explaining human behavior.

By contrast, empathy-based management is based on neuro-science and the results of functional magnetic resonance imaging. We are beginning to understand the behavior of the human brain's highly sophisticated internal mechanics. It is capable of both conscious thought and complex feelings. Both the limbic region and the neocortex of the human brain need to be recognized in order to understand human behavior and create conditions for long-term growth and motivation.

Third, all of Skinner's experiments in optimal conditioning involved artificial conditions. All experimental inducements were forced on animals in a cage. In the real world, our employees do not live in cages without options. Therefore, any smart employee may feel manipulated by the manager's use of carrots and sticks. Forcing an inducement on an employee, rather than on an animal in a cage, may create unintentional negative results. In recent years, because of both advances in brain research and pragmatic empirical shortfalls, behaviorism has fallen out of favor and is being replaced by goal-setting and social-cognitive theories within the field of management.

THEORY #4: HERZBERG, FATHER OF THE TWO-FACTOR THEORY, HYGIENE AND MOTIVATING

Frederick Herzberg's (1923–2000) 1968 publication on two-factor theory has been one of the most reprinted articles in the field of management. Two-factor theory suggests that in terms of motivating employees, there are two separate categories of factors. The first category is called hygiene factors. If absent or neglected, these factors will cause job dissatisfaction for employees. These factors do not motivate employees; rather, they serve only as a source of dissatisfaction if ignored by management, thus the label "hygiene." Hygiene factors include: pay and benefits, job security, fairness of company policy and administration, relationships with coworkers, quality of supervision, and working conditions.

The second category of factors has the ability to motivate workers. These factors include: recognition for accomplishments, promotions, professional growth, increases in responsibility, the work itself. According to Herzberg:

> Despite media attention to the contrary, motivation does not come from perks, plush offices, or even promotions or pay. These extrinsic incentives may stimulate people to put their noses to the grindstone—but they'll likely perform only as long as it takes to get that next raise or promotion.
>
> Most of us are motivated by intrinsic rewards: Interesting, challenging work and the opportunity to achieve and grow into greater responsibility.
>
> Of course, you have to provide some extrinsic incentives. After all, few of us can afford to work for no salary. But the real key to motivating your employees is enabling them to activate their own internal generators. Otherwise, you'll be stuck trying to recharge their batteries yourself—again and again.[33]

Herzberg's understanding of external vs. internal incentives has been the topic of much research over the past four decades

Perspective from Empathy-Based Management

Empathy-based management is highly compatible with Herzberg's two-factor theory. If a manager fails to address the hygiene variables, workers will feel upset or neglected. This will trigger negative emotions in the limbic region of the worker's brain and will lead to job dissatisfaction. The factors Herzberg classifies as motivating factors—including recognition, professional growth, and increased responsibility—give employees hope that their job is improving and hope for a better future. According to empathy-based management, giving people hope is one of the foundations for sustainable worker motivation.

THEORY #5: McGREGOR, FATHER OF THEORIES X AND Y

In 1957, Douglas McGregor (1906–1964) at the MIT Sloan School of Management wrote an article summarizing two distinct management assumptions regarding employee behavior. These two management styles came to be known as theory X and theory Y. A manager who subscribes to theory X believes that employees are inherently lazy and will avoid work whenever possible. The resulting management style is mistrust, close supervision, and strong control systems. By contrast, a manager who has confidence in theory Y believes that workers desire to do well at work. They are self-motivated and have self-control. The theory Y's management style operates in a climate of trust. McGregor encourages managers to examine the positive benefits of utilizing a theory Y management style.

Perspective from Empathy-based Management

It does not matter whether a manager believes in theory X or theory Y, because if the manager's attitudes and actions correspond to his beliefs, he will create a self-fulfilling prophecy. The dispositions and performance of workers *result from* the attitudes of the manager. If the manager believes in theory X and does not trust each employee, the affective portion of each employee's brain will become activated and filled with negative emotions. Poor worker performance will result from the negative attitudes and expectations. If the manager subscribes to theory Y and has confidence in each employee, his attitude will be a source of motivation for employees. It is important to remember that whether a manager believes in his employees or not, the manager is going to affect each employee's level of motivation to work.

THEORY #6: McCLELLAND, FATHER OF MCCLELLAND'S NEEDS THEORY

According to David McClelland (1917–1998), every employee has three distinct needs that are sources of motivation in the work setting: the need for power, the need for achievement, and the need for affiliation. Every person has different needs, but in a work setting, these three needs serve as the greatest source of motivation. To some degree, every person is influenced by the need for power, achievement, and affiliation, but most people are motivated by primarily one of these three needs.

If McClelland were still alive today, he might suggest that empathy-based management fits under the category of the employee's need for affiliation. This is only partially correct; the need for affiliation is only a small part of empathy-based management. Empathy-based management is more concerned with understanding other people, with the ability to calm down emotional states in the human brain so your workers can think clearly on the job. Also, the goals of empathy-based management are to motivate people through giving them hope and a sense of connection and to help them grow both personally and professionally. With hope and professional growth, the worker is motivated to continue growing toward self-actualization and to build a better tomorrow for oneself.

Perspective from Empathy-Based Management

Although McClelland's model of the need for power, achievement, and affiliation is an interesting theory of motivation, unfortunately, the model has severe practical limitations. For example, how much power can a manager give an employee? Can the manager promote the employee to the manager's position or to CEO? And then, what about the next employee who is motivated by power? Likewise, how much recognition can an employee receive? Can the manager give the employee a new trophy every day? Also, for the employee who needs affiliation, how much time should the employee be allowed to spend talking with other employees? As can be surmised, although each employee has needs, managers are limited in what they can do to meet these needs for the purpose of employee motivation. If anything, beyond a model of employee motivation, McClelland's theory may explain why in time an employee outgrows the organization.

THEORY #7: PINK, FATHER OF MOTIVATION 3.0

In his book *Drive: The Surprising Truth About What Motivates Us*, Daniel Pink explains the evolution of worker motivation, but he creates his own nomenclature. The first drive, Motivation 1.0, of human motivation was basic biological survival, namely the need for food, shelter, and clothing. With the industrial revolution and the influential work of Frederick Taylor and B. F. Skinner came "Motivation Operating System 2.0." Motivation 2.0, now standard operating procedure for many organizations, is based on the premise that humans seek rewards and avoid punishments. Mr. Pink demonstrates that motivation strategies based on rewards and punishment work well for motivating employees who perform routine tasks such as assembly line work, but they are not well suited for jobs requiring problem-solving skills.

Thus a reward-and-punishment approach to worker motivation is no longer well suited for corporate America because over the past three decades most assembly-type jobs have been transferred to developing countries. The majority of jobs that remain in the United States require problem-solving skills. The reason that a carrot-and-stick approach to motivation does not work well is because it is designed to control the behavior of people, keeping them subordinate to the corporate agenda. This reward system is designed for compliance. It creates conformity, but at a price of lower creativity.

Motivation strategies based on a carrot-and-stick approach assume work is boring and mundane rather than fun and exciting, and ultimately undermine intrinsic worker motivation. Inducement systems based on external rewards narrow the worker's perspective to focus only on either the reward or punishment, rather than looking for creative and innovative solutions to problems.

Pink writes: "Like all extrinsic motivators, goals narrow our focus. That's one reason they can be effective; they concentrate the mind. But as we've seen, a narrowed focus exacts a cost. For complex or conceptual tasks, offering a reward can blinker the wide-ranging thinking necessary to come up with an innovative solution."[34]

Pink goes on to explain that a reward system signals to your employees that management regards the employee's work to be undesirable, and the worker should regard the job to not be enjoyable.

"In other words, rewards can perform a weird sort of behavioral alchemy: They can transform an interesting task into a drudge. They can turn play into work. And by diminishing intrinsic motivation, they can send performance, creativity, and even upstanding behavior toppling like dominoes."[35]

Therefore, Mr. Pink suggests "motivation 3.0" based on intrinsic motivation, in which he demonstrates that three requirements are responsible for motivating employees: autonomy, purpose, and mastery.

In regard to autonomy, companies often try to control the behavior of employees in order to keep workers on task as they work toward company goals. The opposite work environment of company control is worker autonomy. Given autonomy, workers experience freedom to work toward the goals of their jobs. Workers are their own bosses as they work toward solving a problem or completing a task. With autonomy, one's own reputation and pride is reflected in the quality of one's work.

A second condition for worker motivation is purpose. People who are working for a cause that is important to them or stands for something that contributes to improving humanity are significantly more motivated than workers who are simply doing a job.

The third force responsible for employee motivation is mastery. It is human nature to desire to excel at something. Whether practicing a musical instrument or a sport, or solving a puzzle or a video game, people of all ages spend hours trying to master something that is important to them. Along with autonomy and purpose, the desire to master one's profession drives people's intrinsic motivation. Daniel Pink summarizes his theory: "The science shows that the secret to high performance isn't our biological drive or our reward-and-punishment drive, but our third drive—our deep-seated desire to direct our own lives, to extend and expand our abilities, and to make a contribution."[36]

Perspective from Empathy-Based Management

Daniel Pink successfully analyzes the three variables necessary for intrinsic worker motivation to occur. Mr. Pink lays the foundation from which one can understand the need for empathy-based management. But because a worker's motivation is intrinsic in Pink's framework, the manager plays a passive rather than an active role in supervising employees. The manager's role includes a move away from traditional motivation methods, including carrots-and-sticks types of inducements. By handing over control and giving employees more autonomy, the supervisor fosters an environment conducive to professional development and mastery.

By contrast, empathy-based management advocates an active

role for managers. The active role does not mean controlling employees, but rather to have an active, supportive relationship with each employee. This personal relationship between the manager and each employee is useful for removing barriers and distractions in each worker's life and creating a more conducive work environment. In a collegial, supportive work environment, each employee in the organization can realize purpose, and pursue autonomy and mastery. More specifically, managers assume an active, personal relationship with each employee by removing barriers in each person's life, giving them hope and calming negative emotions when they flare, so that each worker can use the cognitive side of his brain to problem solve and make progress toward mastery (professional growth). In other words, Pink's work explains the "what" required for employee motivation; empathy-based management explains the "how to" managers go about achieving employee motivation.

Appendix B

CHARACTERISTICS OF A MENTOR

Jim Warner and Kaley Klemp[37] remind us of the characteristics that every worker is looking for in a mentor. For your own professional growth as a supervisor, aim to incorporate the following characteristics into your management style:

Characteristics of mentors:

- They have a way of being that you admire. They walk their talk.
- Their lives are grounded in honesty, compassion, patience, and discipline.
- They are neither intimidated nor intimidating.
- They have the wisdom to know when to stay in the background and let things unfold, and when to be decisive in the moment.
- They have a highly developed intuition.
- They can conceive new approaches to fit an emerging situation.
- They can quickly get to the heart of problems and speak the hard truths.

- They can "hold the space" for you to express your thoughts and emotions safely.
- They treat confidentiality as sacred.
- They are committed to their own ongoing personal growth and holistic health.
- They have their own "personal advisory board" for guidance and accountability.
- When they drift into unproductive behaviors, they shift back quickly with integrity.
- They take themselves lightly; they can laugh at themselves.

For anyone interested in Warner and Klemp's work regarding mentorship in the office, I encourage you to read their book: *The Drama-Free Office: A Guide to Healthy Collaborations with Your Team, Coworkers, and Boss* ©2011.

Appendix C

MANAGING BY FEAR VS.
MANAGING BY EMPATHY

Based on outdated prescriptions for effective management practices, often managers think that they have to be tough in order to motivate employees to work hard. The purpose of this short appendix is to present and contrast the results of managing by fear vs. managing with empathy.

Results of Managing by Fear

The management practice of using fear in order to motivate subordinates is still an often-used tactic in both industry and athletics. Although this practice may appear to be a catalyst for short-term motivation, let us take a look at the overall effects of this motivational technique.

- The manager instills a sense of fear into each employee.
- Yields effective short-term results.
- Employees feel obligated to work hard.
- This sense of obligation results in angry employees.
- The limbic region in the employee's brain is triggered into a fight-or-flight response.

- The fight-or-flight response shuts down cognitive processes in the employee's brain, and she can no longer think in order to problem solve.
- The employee's heart and soul are not engaged.
- The employee is compliant but not committed.
- The employee's focus is on being angry at her boss.
- No personal relationship can form between the manager and the employee.
- The employee does not trust or respect his boss.
- The manager is required to continually monitor and control the employee's behavior.
- The manager cannot ask for creative ideas from the employees.
- The manager is required to do all of the problem solving and decision making.
- The manager must continuously monitor each employee's work ethic.
- The manager cannot trust the employees in an emergency.
- The employees have no loyalty to either the manager or the organization.
- The employees will not problem solve, a skill required for most industries today.

Therefore, overall we see that management through fear is not a viable strategy for long-term employee motivation.

Results of Managing with Empathy

Now for contrast, let us now examine the effectiveness of using empathy to motivate your employees:

With empathy, the manager has unconditional positive regard for each employee, and each employee feels unconditionally accepted. The employee feels the manager's understanding, unconditional acceptance, and encouragement. Each employee has a supportive personal relationship with the manager.

- The work environment is emotionally and physically safe.

- Employees are polite, competent, and enjoyable coworkers.

- The limbic region in each employee's brain is calm and stable.

- The cognitive portion of each worker's brain is fully engaged.

- Each employee can problem solve and make decisions.

- Each employee's heart and soul are engaged.

- The employee is loyal to her manager and committed to the organization.

- Employees volunteer ideas as they problem solve.

- The manager can focus on his job, rather than on employee compliance.

- Employees enjoy their work.

- The work environment is conducive for personal and professional employee growth.

- Personal and professional growth results in rising self-efficacy.

By using empathy and from the resulting professional growth that occurs, long-term employee motivation becomes feasible.[38]

Appendix D

MANAGEMENT BY SHAME

Some organizations attempt to control employee behavior through shame. Managing employees through shaming them is perhaps the most destructive behavior a manager can do to his employees. For a manager to suggest guilt is to suggest the employee is a good person who made a mistake in one area of his life. By contrast, to shame a person is to suggest the employee is worthless and unfixable. Shaming experiences result in a significant distortion of one's self-perception. Over time, living within a shaming environment can lead to serious personal and emotional problems through the continual experience of internalized humiliation.

According to Kaufman, in *The Psychology of Shame*:

> Shame is the affect of inferiority. No other affect is more central to the development of identity. None is closer to the experienced self, nor more disturbing. Shame is felt as an inner torment. It is the most poignant experience of the self by the self, whether felt in the humiliation of cowardice, or in the sense of failure to cope successfully with a challenge. Shame is a wound made from the inside, dividing us from both ourselves and others.
>
> Whether all eyes are upon us or only our own, we feel fundamentally deficient as individuals, diseased, defective . . . The excruciating observation of the self that results, this torment of self-consciousness, becomes so acute as to create a binding, almost paralyzing effect.[39]

Also explained by Silvan Tomkins:

> If distress is the affect of suffering, shame is the affect of indignity, of defeat, of transgression and of alienation. Though terror speaks to life and death and distress makes of the world a vale of tears, yet shame strikes deepest into the heart of man. While terror and distress hurt, they are wounds inflicted from outside which penetrate the smooth surface of the ego; but shame is felt as an inner torment, a sickness of the soul. It does not matter whether the humiliated one has been shamed by derisive laughter or whether he mocks himself. In either event he feels himself naked, defeated, alienated, lacking in dignity or worth.[40]

The inability to escape shaming experiences, including a shaming work environment, results in severe psychological damage in the way the recipient views himself as a person. The recipient starts to view himself as a diminished human being, rather than as a valuable, whole, intact, coherent person. Long-term exposure to being shamed contributes to mental health issues, including depression and self-destructive behaviors. As explained by Kaufman:

> This binding effect of shame is central to understanding shame's impact on personality development. The binding effects of exposure, of feeling seen, acutely disturb the smooth functioning of the self. Exposure binds movement and speech, paralyzing the self. The urge to hide, to disappear, is a spontaneous reaction to the self's heightened visibility; it can overwhelm the self. To feel shame is to feel inherently bad, fundamentally flawed as a person.
>
> Shame is an affective experience that violates both interpersonal trust and internal security. Intense shame is a sickness with the self, a disease of the spirit.[41]

In other words, please avoid shaming your employees at all cost. While empathy aims to build up your employee in order to create an environment for professional growth, shame aims to tear down the employee in order to create an atmosphere of compliance.

Appendix E

Ego and empathy have direct opposite foci. Ego focuses on the feelings and needs of oneself. Empathy is concerned with the feelings and needs of another person.

Organization Based on "Ego" of Management

I. Hierarchy

- Feeling of superiority

- Focus on money, appearance, and power

- Set boundaries to protect management

- Psychological barriers exist between manager and subordinates, erected by the manager

- Subordinates cannot alter this barrier; only the manager can erect and dismantle the barrier

II. World of Judging Others

- World of judging people as "a success" or "a failure"

- Failure = rejection

- Cannot see beyond one's own needs to see the needs of others, including employee's needs and feelings
- World of punishment

III. Purpose of the Employee is to Serve the Top, or to Serve Management

- World of attempting to control and program employee behavior
- World of employee assimilation
- Gives the message: "We don't care about you"
- Results in employee apathy and fear
- The limbic region of the employee's brain overrides the cognitive portions, resulting in no critical thinking and problem solving, only obligatory compliance

IV. Results

- Employees' attitudes reflecting negative emotions, and no loyalty, inspiration or positive employee energy

Organization Based on Empathetic Management

I. World of Interaction

- Top = mature leader or mentor, looking for tomorrow's leaders in the company
- Top invests in the personal and professional growth of each employee
- Boundaries are set to protect everyone in the organization

II. World of Mentoring, Rather Than Judging

- No success or failure, only a world of learning and growth
- No punishment, only consequences
- Investment in the next generation

III. Purpose of the Top

- Service to all organizational stakeholders, especially customers and employees
- Every stakeholder is viewed as a unique individual
- Each individual has distinctive capabilities and contributions to the organization
- Gives the message: "You are highly valued, both as a person and as an employee"

IV. Results

- Removal of fear leaves employees feeling secure, with stable emotions and allows employees to make decisions and solve problems.
- Loyalty and productivity both increase.
- New ideas and new innovations are created as employees grow personally and professionally, increasing profitability.
- The organization is an enjoyable place to work.

Appendix F

NARCISSISM VS. LOVE
FOR OTHER PEOPLE

Narcissism, or self-infatuation, of individuals in positions of management can be found in many organizations today. Gary Latham has written in detail on the topic of narcissistic behavior. According to Latham:

> Narcissists have an extreme emotional investment in establishing their superiority, even if they are unsure whether their feelings of superiority are merited. The grandiosity associated with narcissism acts as a defense against having an unfavorable self-image as well as the feelings of failure that accompany it. Because narcissists are vulnerable to ego-threatening information, they are vigilant for opportunities to find ways to maintain their sense of superiority over others. They seek ways to defend their ego against unfavorable evaluative information, particularly against data that are factual and accurate. Threats to their ego quickly elicit their anger and aggression toward the source of the evaluation. They tend to derogate the evaluator and the appraisal instrument as well as innocent third parties. The primary purpose of their aggression is to punish the evaluator and to reaffirm their dominance over the person, thereby achieving an "ego boost" to lessen the impact of the threat to their ego. This is because information that undermines beliefs central to the definition of self is intolerable for highly narcissistic individuals.[42]

Individuals who display narcissistic behaviors while employed in management positions are a common occurrence. This manifestation of narcissistic behavior today in corporate America is rather unfortunate. A manager who displays narcissistic tendencies is a liability to both his/her subordinates, and to the organization as a whole.

By comparison, love for other people can be beneficial to everyone in your organization. Here's a description of love for other people from the book of 1 Corinthians, chapter 13, verses 4–7 of the Christian Bible (New International Version): "Love is patient, love is kind. It does not envy, it does not boast, it is not proud. It does not dishonor others, it is not self-seeking, it is not easily angered, it keeps no record of wrongs. Love does not delight in evil but rejoices with the truth. It always protects, always trusts, always hopes, always perseveres."

In other words, a manager who displays acts of "love" or kindness toward one's subordinate creates an environment of safety, acceptance, and understanding. When you encounter an empathetic manager, you will recognize the second set of attributes, described as love for other people, are also attributes of an emotionally healthy person.

Questions for Thought

1. As an employee, what emotions would one have working for a narcissistic manager? What feelings would one have working for a loving manager in his treatment of employees?

2. In each case, how would the resulting emotions affect your employee's motivation to work?

Worksheet #1

DAILY NOTES AND IMPORTANT DETAILS FOR EACH EMPLOYEE

Today's Date _____

Self

This morning, my own mood is:

_____

This morning, when I woke up, my mind was concerned about or focused on:

_____

Employee #1 Name: _____

This morning, the mood of my employee was:

_____

My employee brought up these issues:

_____

Together, we resolved the issue(s), by agreeing on:

_____

Something new I learned about my employee today:

_____

Employee #2 Name: _____

This morning, the mood of my employee was:

_____

My employee brought up these issues:

_____

Together, we resolved the issue(s), by agreeing on:

_____

Something new I learned about my employee today:

_____

Employee #3 Name: _____

This morning, the mood of my employee was:

_____

My employee brought up these issues:

_____

Together, we resolved the issue(s), by agreeing on:

_____

Something new I learned about my employee today:

_____

Worksheet #2

THE FIVE STEPS OF THE INTERSUBJECTIVE EXPERIENCE

Today's Date _____

Following are the five steps of the intersubjective experience when something is bothering your employee:

Step 1: Your employee raises an issue with you. Ask questions to learn your employee's interpretation of the event.

Step 2: Respond with empathy (e.g., "That was a horrible thing that happened to you").

Step 3: Investigate the motives your employee attributes to the person(s) who caused the event (e.g., "So why do you think this even happened?").

Step 4: Respond with empathy (e.g., "Oh, now I understand what you are saying.").

Step 5: Clarify your employee's point of view. Together, you and your employee cocreate new meaning and understanding to the event and look for a possible solution. (e.g., How can we resolve this problem so it does not happen again?" or "Because we have been served lemons, how can we make lemonade?").

Notes regarding the problem, this employee, other people involved, and course of action moving forward:

_____

_____

_____

_____

_____

_____

_____

_____

_____

Worksheet #3

EMPATHETIC CHOICES MODEL

Today's Date _____

Use the empathetic choices model to help your employees solve their own problems.

There are either three or five steps to the *empathetic choices model*, depending on the decision-making ability of each employee.

Step 1: Your employee explains his problem. Offer an empathetic response to her problem (e.g., "That is horrible.").

Step 2: Ask how your employee plans to respond (e.g., "What are you going to do to solve your problem?").

Step 3A: If the employee's solution sounds reasonable, affirm the employee's choice with empathy (e.g., "Sounds like you have things figured out; go for it!").

OR

Step 3B: If the employee's solution is unacceptable, unrealistic, or will not work, in response, offer your employee several acceptable choices (e.g., "Would you like to hear what I might suggest?").

Step 4: Make sure the employee understands the consequences of each choice (e.g., "So what might happen if you decide to . . . ?").

Step 5: Give the employee permission to make a decision and live with the consequences (e.g., "Sounds good, let me know how things go for you.").

Notes regarding the problem, this employee, and agreed-upon course of action moving forward:

_____

_____

_____

_____

_____

_____

_____

_____

ABOUT THE AUTHOR

George Langelett is a professor of management and economics at South Dakota State University in Brookings, SD. He teaches classes in management, small business management, human resource management, marketing research, and macroeconomics. He grew up in Thief River Falls, MN, and attended the University of Northwestern in St. Paul, MN, where he earned his BS in marketing. In 2000 he graduated from the University of Nebraska with a PhD in economics. His dissertation focused on human capital formation and economic growth. While in Lincoln, he met his wife, Lara, and has been happily married for twelve years.

While initially interested in the economic benefits of human capital formation, over time Dr. Langelett became more interested in researching the causes and impediments to human motivation. In his words: "As an economist, as well as professor of management, an enduring issue that needs to be better understood is: why are some people significantly more productive than other people? Ultimately, what can a manager do to motivate each employee and help them reach their potential?" Being dissatisfied with orthodox textbook prescriptions, Dr. Langelett has devoted his research to finding answers that are compatible with findings from other fields, particularly neuroscience, and also the simple reality of "what actually works? And why?" Knowing that research is an ongoing endeavor, Dr. Langelett enjoys discussing human motivation with supervisors and managers from all types of organizations as well as researchers from a variety of academic disciplines.

NOTES

1 Michael Jacobs, "How Business Schools Have Failed Business," *Wall Street Journal*, April 24, 2009, http://online.wsj.com/news/articles/SB.

2 Dev Patnaik and Peter Mortensen, *Wired to Care: How Companies Prosper When They Create Widespread Empathy* (Saddle River, NJ: FT Press, 2009).

3 "Empathy," Dictionary.com, accessed January 10, 2014, http://dictionary.reference.com/browse/empathy?s=ts.

4 Carl Rogers, *On Becoming a Person* (New York, NY: Houghton Mifflin, 1961), 332.

5 "Empathy in Leadership – 10 Reasons Why It Matters," Tanveer Naseer, accessed January 10, 2014, http://www.tanveernaseer.com/why-empathy-matters-in-leadership/.

6 Arthur P. Ciaramicoli and Katherine Ketcham, *The Power of Empathy* (New York: Dutton, 2000).

7 Job 2:11–13, New International Version.

8 "Sympathy," Dictionary.com, accessed January 10, 2014, http://dictionary.reference.com/browse/sympathy?s=t.

9 Ciaramicoli and Ketcham, *The Power of Empathy*.

10 Andrew Curran, *The Little Book of Big Stuff About the Human Brain*, ed. Ian Gilbert (Trowbridge, Wilshire, UK: Crown House Publishing, 2008), 2.

11 Ibid., 26.

12 Daniel Pink, *Drive: The Surprising Truth About What Motivates Us* (New York: Penguin Group, 2009), 48.

13 Ibid., 43.

14 Mark Hickson, III and Christie Beck, "Genetic, Neurological, and Social Bases of Empathy," *Human Communications* 11, no. 3 (2008): 359–382.

15 Curran, *Little Book of Big Stuff*, 26.

16 Patnaik and Mortensen, *Wired to Care*, 115.

17 "Empathy in Leadership," Naseer.

18 Patnaik and Mortensen, *Wired to Care*, 143.

19 "Empathy: Leadership Strength Or Weakness?" Marcia Moran, Positive Business DC, March 20, 2013, http://positivebusinessdc.com/empathy-leadership-strength-or-weakness/.

20 "Stress," Merriam-Webster, accessed January 10, 2014, http://www.merriam-webster.com/dictionary/stress.

21 Noel Tichy and Sherman Stratford, *Control Your Destiny or Someone Else Will* (New York: Currency Doubleday, 1993), 251.

22 John Baldoni, *Great Motivation Secrets of Great Leaders* (New York: McGraw-Hill, 2005), 196.

23 Anne Bruce and James Pepitone, *Motivating Employees* (New York: McGraw-Hill, 1999), 81.

24 Xavier Amador, *I Am Not Sick, I Don't Need Help* (Peconic, NY: Vida Press, 2010), 118.

25 Daniel Hughes, *Attachment-Focused Family Therapy* (New York: W.W. Norton, 2007), 19.

26 Ibid., 21.

27 Daniel G. Amen, *Making a Good Brain Great* (New York: Random House, 2005), 148.

28 Gershen Kaufman, *The Psychology of Shame, 2nd Edition: Theory and Treatment of Shame-Based Syndromes* (New York: Springer Press, 1996), 24.

29 Ciaramicoli and Ketcham, *The Power of Empathy*, 153.

30 Baldoni, *Great Motivation Secrets*, 151.

31 John Bowlby, *A Secure Base* (New York: Basic Books, 1998), 121.

32 Baldoni, *Great Motivation Secrets*, 53.

33 Frederick Herzberg, *One More Time, How Do You Motivate Employees?* (Boston, MA: Harvard Business School Publishing Company, 2008), 61–62.

34 Pink, *Drive*, 48.

35 Ibid., 35.

36 Ibid., 144.

37 Jim Warner and Kaley Klemp, *The Drama-Free Office: A Guide to Healthy Collaborations with Your Team, Coworkers, and Boss* (Austin, TX: Greenleaf Press, 2011), 96.

38 Underlying principles related to fear and empathy were adopted from The Love and Logic Institute, Inc., Golden, CO, © Jim Fay, Foster Cline, and Charles Fay.

39 Kaufman, *Psychology of Shame*, 16–18.

40 Silvan Tomkins, *Affect Imagery Consciousness: The Negative Affects*, vol. 2 (New York: Springer, 1963), 118.

41 Kaufman, *Psychology of Shame*, 18.

42 Gary Latham, *Work Motivation: History, Theory, Research, and Practice* (Thousand Oaks, CA: Sage Publications, 2007), 247.

BIBLIOGRAPHY

Amador, Xavier. *I Am Not Sick, I Don't Need Help*. Peconic, NY: Vida Press, 2010.

Amen, Daniel G. *Making a Good Brain Great*. New York: Random House, 2005.

Baldoni, John. *Great Motivation Secrets of Great Leaders*. New York: McGraw-Hill, 2005.

Bowlby, John. *A Secure Base*. New York: Basic Books, 1998.

Bruce, Anne and James Pepitone. *Motivating Employees*. New York: McGraw-Hill, 1999.

Ciaramicoli, Arthur P. and Katherine Ketcham. *The Power of Empathy*. New York: Dutton, 2000.

Curran, Andrew. *The Little Book of Big Stuff About the Human Brain*. Edited by Ian Gilbert. Trowbridge, Wilshire, UK: Crown House Publishing, 2008.

Damasio, Antonio. *Descartes' Error: Emotion, Reason, and the Human Brain*. New York: Avon Books, 1994.

Dictionary.com. "Empathy." Accessed January 10, 2014. http://dictionary.reference.com/browse/empathy?s=ts.

Dictionary.com. "Sympathy." Accessed January 10, 2014. http://dictionary.reference.com/browse/sympathy?s=t.

Herzberg, Frederick. *One More Time, How Do You Motivate Employees?* Boston, MA: Harvard Business School Publishing Company, 2008.

Hickson, Mark, III, and Christie Beck. "Genetic, Neurological, and Social Bases of Empathy." *Human Communications* 11, no. 3 (2008).

Hughes, Daniel. *Attachment-Focused Family Therapy*. New York: W.W. Norton, 2007.

Jacobs, Michael. "How Business Schools Have Failed Business." *Wall Street Journal*. April 24, 2009. http://online.wsj.com/news/articles/SB.

Kaufman, Gershen. *The Psychology of Shame, 2nd Edition: Theory and Treatment of Shame-Based Syndromes.* New York: Springer Press, 1996.

Latham, Gary. *Work Motivation: History, Theory, Research, and Practice.* Thousand Oaks, CA: Sage Publications, 2007.

McClelland, David. "Achievement Motivation can be Developed." Harvard Business Review, 43, pp. 6–24.

Merriam-Webster. "Stress." Accessed January 10, 2014. http://www.merriam-webster.com/dictionary/stress.

Moran, Marcia. "Empathy: Leadership Strength Or Weakness?" Positive Business DC. March 20, 2013. http://positivebusinessdc.com/empathy-leadership-strength-or-weakness/.

Naseer, Tanveer. "Empathy in Leadership – 10 Reasons Why It Matters." Accessed January 10, 2014. http://www.tanveernaseer.com/why-empathy-matters-in-leadership/.

Patnaik, Dev and Peter Mortensen. *Wired to Care: How Companies Prosper When They Create Widespread Empathy.* Saddle River, NJ: FT Press, 2009.

Pink, Daniel. *Drive: The Surprising Truth About What Motivates Us.* New York: Penguin Group, 2009.

Rogers, Carl. *On Becoming a Person.* New York: Houghton Mifflin, 1961.

Siegel, Daniel. *The Developing Mind: How Relationship and the Brain Interact to Shape Who We Are.* New York: Guilford Press, 1999.

Taylor, Frederick Winslow. *The Principles of Scientific Management.* New York: Harper & Row, 1911.

Tichy, Noel and Sherman Stratford. *Control Your Destiny or Someone Else Will.* New York: Currency Doubleday, 1993.

Tomkins, Silvan. *Affect Imagery Consciousness: The Negative Affects, vol. 2.* New York: Springer, 1963.

Warner, Jim and Kaley Klemp. *The Drama-Free Office: A Guide to Healthy Collaborations with Your Team, Coworkers, and Boss.* Austin, TX: Greenleaf Press, 2011.

RECOMMENDED
FURTHER READING

Abercrombie, H. C., Schaefer, S. M., Larson, C. L., Oakes, T. R., Lindgren, K. A., Holden, E., et al. (1998). Metabolic rate in the right amygdala predicts negative affect in depressed patients. *Neuroreport*, 9, 3301–3307.

Adams, J. S. (1963). Toward an understanding of inequity. *Journal of Abnormal and Social Psychology*, 67, 422–436.

Adolphs, R. (2002). Neural systems for recognizing emotion. *Current Opinion in Neurobiology*, 12 (2), 169–177.

Adolphs, R. (2002). Trust in the brain. *Nature Neuroscience*, 5, 192–193.

Adolphs, R. (2006). How do we know the minds of others? Domain-specificity, simulation, and enactive social cognition. *Brain Research*, 1079, 25–35.

Adolphs, R., & Tranel, D. (2004). Impaired judgment of sadness but not happiness following bi-lateral amygdala damage. *Journal of Cognitive Neuroscience*, 16, 453–462.

Adolphs, R., Tranel, D., & Damasio, A. R. (1998). The human amygdala in social judgment. *Nature*, 393, 470–474.

Ainsworth, M. D. S., Blehar, J. C., Waters, E., & Wall, S. (1978). *Patterns of attachment: A psychological study of the strange situation*. Hillsdale, NJ: Erlbaum.

Amabile, Teresa M., Elise Phillips, and Mary Ann Collins, (1993). Person and Environmental in Talent Development: The Case of Creativity, in *Talent Development: Proceedings from the 1993 Henry B. and Jocelyn Wallace National Research Symposium on Talent Development*, edited by Nicolas Colangelo, Susan G. Assouline, an DeAnn L. Ambroson Dayton: Ohio Psychology Press, 273–274.

Amaral, D. G., Price, J. L., Pitkanen, A., & Carmichael, S. T. (1992). Anatomical organization of the primate amygdaloid complex. In J. P. Aggleton (Ed.), *The amygdala: Neurobiological aspects of emotion, memory, and mental dysfunction* (pp. 1–66). New York: Wiley.

Amedi, A., Merabet, L. B., Bermpohl, F., & Pascual-Leone, A. (2005). The occipital cortex in the blind: Lessons about plasticity and vision. *Current Directions in Psychological Science*, 14, (6), 306–311.

Amodio, D. M., & Frith, C. D. (2006). Meeting of minds: The medial frontal cortex and social cognition. *Nature Reviews Neuroscience*, 7(4), 268–277.

Armory, J. L., Corbo, V., Clement, M. H., & Brunet, A. (2005). Amygdala response in patients with acute PTSD to masked and unmasked emotional facial expressions. *American Journal of Psychiatry*, 162, 1960–1963.

Augustine, J. R. (1996). Circuitry and functional aspects of the insular lobe in primates including humans. *Brain Research Reviews*, 22, 229–244.

Avenanti, A., Bueti, D., Galati, G., & Aglioti, S. M. (2005). Transcranial magnetic stimulation highlights the sensorimotor side of empathy for pain. *Nature Neuroscience*, 8, 955–960.

Averill, J. R. (1982). *Anger and aggression: An essay on emotion*. New York: Springer.

Badenoch, B. (2008). *Being a Brain Wise Therapist: A Practical Guide to Interpersonal Neurobiology*. New York: W.W. Norton.

Baer, R.A., Smith, G. T., Hopkins, J., Krietemeyer, J., & Toney, L. (2006). Using self-report assessment methods to explore facets of mindfulness. *Assessment*, 13(1), 27–45.

Baird A.A., Gruber, S. A., Fein, D. A., Steinfard, R. J., Renshaw, P. F. & Yurgelun-Todd, D. A. (1999). Functional magnetic resonance imaging of facial affect recognition in children and adolescents. *Journal of the American Academy of Child and Adolescent Psychiatry*, 38(2) 195–199.

Bandura, A. (1988). Organizational application of social cognitive theory. *Australian Journal of Management*, 13(2), pp. 275–302.

Barak, A., Engle, C., Katzir, L., & Fisher, W. A. (1987). Increasing the level of empathic understanding by means of a game. *Simulation and Games*, 18, 458–470.

Bargh, J. A., Chen, M., & Burrows, L. (1996). Automaticity of social behavior: Direct effects of trait construct and stereotype-activation on action. *Journal of Personality and Social Psychology*, 71, 230–244.

Barrett-Lennard, G. T. (1993). The phases and focus of empathy. *British Journal of Medical Psychology*, 66, 3–14.

Barrett-Lennard, G. T. (1997). The recovery of empathy: Toward others and self. In A. C. Bohart & L. S. Greenberg (Eds.), *Empathy reconsidered: New directions in psychotherapy* (pp. 103–121). Washington, DC: American Psychological Association.

Basch, M. F. (1983). Empathic understanding: A review of the concept and some theoretical considerations. *Journal of the American Psychoanalytic Association*, 31, 101–1265.

Batson, C. D., Batson, J. G., Slings by, J. K., Harrell, K. L., Peekna, H. M., & Todd, R. M. (1991). "Empathic joy and the empathy-altruism hypothesis." *Journal of Personality and Social Psychology*, 61, 413–426.

Batson, C. D., Early, S., & Salvarini, G. (1997). Perspective taking: Imagining how another feels versus imagining how you would feel. *Personality and Social Personality Bulletin*, 23, 751–758.

Bavelas, J. B., Black, A., Lemery, C. R., & Mullett, J. (1987). Motor mimicry as primitive empathy. In N. Eisenbery & J. Strayer (Eds.), *Empathy and its development* (pp.317–338). Cambridge: Cambridge University Press.

Bavelas, J. B., Black, A., Lemery, C. R., & Mullett, J. (1996). I show you how you feel: Motor mimicry as a communicative act. *Journal of Personality and Social Psychology*, 50, 322–329.

Begley, S. (2007). *Train your mind, change your brain.: How a new science reveals our extraordinary potential to transform ourselves.* New York: Ballantine.

Berthoz, S., Armony, J., Blair, R. J. R., & Dolan, R. (2002). Neural correlates of violation of social norms and embarrassment. *Brain*, 125 (8), 1696–1708.

Birbaumer, N., Viet, R., Lotze, M., Erb. M., Hermann, C., Grodd, W., & Flor, H. (2005). Deficient fear conditioning in psychopathy: A functional magnetic resonance imaging study. *Archives of General Psychiatry*, 62 (7), 799–805.

Björkqvist, K., Österman, K., & Kaukiainen, A. (2000). Social intelligence – empathy = aggression? *Aggression and Violent Behavior*, 5, 191–200.

Black, H., & Phillips, S. (1982). An intervention program for the development of empathy in student teachers. *Journal of Psychology*, 112, 159–168.

Blair, K. S., Marsh, A. A., Morton, J., Vythilingham, M., Jones, M., Mondillo, K., Pine, D. S., Drevets, W. C., & Blair, R. J. R. (2006). Choosing the lesser of two evils, the better of two goods: Specifying the roles of ventromedial prefrontal cortex and dorsal anterior cingulate cortex in object choice. *Journal of Neuroscience*, 26 (44). 11379–11386.

Blair, R. J. R. (2004). The roles of orbital frontal cortex in the modulation of antisocial behavior. *Brain and Cognition*, 55 (1), 198–208.

Blair, R. J. R., Colledge, E., Murray, L., & Mitchell, D. G. (2001). A selective impairment in the processing of sad and fearful expressions in children with psychopathic tendencies. *Journal of Abnormal Child Psychology*, 29 (6), 491–498.

Blair, R. J. R., Jones, L., Clark, F., & Smith, M. (1997). The psychopathic individual: A lack of responsiveness to distress cues? *Psychophysiology*, 34, 192–198.

Blair, R. J. R., Mitchell, D. G. V., & Blair, K. S. (2005). *The psychopath: Emotion and the brain*. Oxford: Blackwell.

Bliss T.V.P., & Collingridge G.L. (1993). A synaptic model of memory–long-term potentiation in the hippocampus. *Nature*, 361, 31–9

Bohart, A. C. (2003). Person-centered psychotherapy and related experiential approaches. In A. S. Gurman & S. B. Messer (Eds.), *Essential psychotherapies: Theory and practice* (2nd ed., pp. 107–148). New York: Guilford Press.

Bohart, A. C., Elliott, R., Greenberg, L. S., & Watson, J. C. (2002). Empathy. In J. C. Norcross (Ed.), *Psychotherapy relationships that work: Therapist contributions and responsiveness to patient needs* (pp. 89–108). New York: Oxford University Press.

Bohart, A. C., & Greenberg, L. S. (1997). *Empathy reconsidered: New directions in psychotherapy*. Washington, DC: American Psychological Association.

Botvinick, M., Jha, A. P., Bylsma, L. M., Fabian, S. A., Solomon, P. E., & Prkachin, K. M. (2005). Viewing facial expressions of pain engages cortical areas involved in the direct experience of pain. *NeuroImage*, 25, 312–319.

Bowen, M. (1983). *Attachment*. New York: Basic Books. (Original work published 1969).

Bowen, M. (1994). *Family therapy in clinical practice*. New York: Ballantine.

Bozarth, J.D. (1997). Empathy from the framework of client-centered theory and the Rogerian hypothesis. In A. Bohart & L. S. Greenberg (Eds.), *Empathy reconsidered: New directions in psychotherapy* (pp. 81–102). Washington, DC: American Psychological Association.

Bozarth, J. D. (1999). *Person-centered therapy: A revolutionary paradigm* (2nd ed.). Ross-on-Wye, UK: PCCS Books.

Bozarth, J. D., Zimring, F. M., & Tausch, R. (2002). Client-centered therapy: The evolution of a revolution. In D. J. Cain & J. Semman (Eds.), *Humanistic psychotherapies: Handbook of research and practice* (pp. 147–188). Washington, DC: American Psychological Association.

Bremner, J. D., Randall, R., Scott, T., Branen, R., Seibyl, J., Southwick, S., et al (1995). MRI-based measurement of hippocampal volume in patients with combat-related posttraumatic stress disorder. *American Journal of Psychiatry*, 152, 973–981.

Bremner, J.D., Randall, P., Vermetten, E. Staib, L., Bronen R., Mazure, C., et al. (1997). Magnetic resonance imaging-based measurement of Hippocampal volume in the post traumatic system disorder related to children hood physical and sexual abuse: A preliminary report. *Biological Psychiatry*, 41, 23–32.

Brioni, J.D., Nagahara, A.H., McGaugh, J.L. (1989). Involvement of the amygdala GABAergic system in the modulation of memory storage. *Brain Res*, 487, 105–12.

Brothers, L. (1989). A biological perspective on empathy. *American Journal of Psychiatry*, 146, 10–19.

Brown, H. (August 25, 2005). A brain in the head, and one in the gut. *New York Times*. Retrieved from http://www.nytimes.com/2005/08/24/health/24iht-snbrain.html.

Buccino, G., Vogt, S., Ritzl, A., Fink, G. R., Zilles, K., Freund, H. J., & Rizzolatti, G. (2004). Neural circuits underlying imitation learning of hand actions: An event-related fMRI study. *Neuron*, 42 (2), 323–334.

Buck, R., & Ginsburg, B. (1997). Communicative genes and the evolution of empathy. In W. Ickes (Ed.), *Empathic accuracy*. New York: Guilford.

Buckner, R. L., Andrews-Hanna, J. R., & Schacter, D. L. (2008). The brain's default network: Anatomy, function, and relevance to disease. *Annals of the New York Academy of Sciences*, 1124, 1–38. doi:10.1196/annuals. 1440.011.

Budhani, S., Marsh, A. A., Pine, D. S., & Blair, R. J. (2007). Neural correlates of response reversal: Considering acquisition. *NeuroImage*, 34 (4), 1754–1765.

Burke, K. (1966). *Language as symbolic interaction: Essays on life, literature, and method*. Berkeley, CA: University of California Press.

Burns, D. D., & Nolen-Hoeksema, S. (1992). Therapeutic empathy and recovery from depression in cognitive-behavioral therapy: A structural equation model. *Journal of Consulting and Clinical Psychology*, 60, 441–449.

Cacioppo, J. T., Hughes, M. E., Waite, L. J., Hawkely, L. C., & Thisted, R. A. (2006). Loneliness as a specific risk factor for depressive symptoms: Cross-sectional and longitudinal analysis. *Psychology of Aging*, 21, 140–151.

Cahill L. (2000). Neurobiological mechanisms of emotionally influenced, long-term memory. *Prog Brain Res* 126:29–37.

Cahill L., McGaugh J.L. (1996). The neurobiology of memory for emotional events: adrenergic activation and the amygdala. *Proc West Pharmacol Soc*, 39, 81–4.

Cahill, L., Prins, B., Weber, M., McGaugh, J.L. (1994). Beta-adrenergic activation and memory for emotional events. *Nature*, 371, 702–4.

Cannon-Bowers, J. A., Salas, E., & Converse, S. (1993). Shared mental models in expert team decision making. In N. J. Castellan, Jr. (Ed.), *Individual and group decision making: Current issues* (pp. 221–246). Hillsdale, NJ: Erlbaum.

Carr, L., Iacoboni, M., Dubeau, M. C., Mazziotta, J. C., & Lenzi, G. L. (2003). Neural mechanisms of empathy in humans: A relay from neural systems for imitation to limbic areas. *Proceedings of the National Academy of Sciences of USA*, 100 (9), 5497–5502.

Carter, C. S. (2003). Developmental consequences of oxytocin. *Physiology and Behavior*, 79, 383–397.

Carter, S. C., Harris, J., & Porges, S. W. (2009). Neural and evolutionary perspectives on empathy. In J. Decety & W. Ickes (Eds.), *The social neuroscience of empathy* (pp. 169–182). Cambridge, MA: MIT Press.

Chakrabarti, B., & Baron-Cohen, S. (2006). Empathizing: Neurocognitive developmental mechanisms and individual differences. *Progress in Brain Research*, 156, 403–417.

Charbonneau, D., & Nicol, A. A. M. (2002). Emotional intelligence and prosocial behaviors in adolescents. *Psychological Reports*, 90, 361–370.

Chartrand, T. L., & Bargh, J. A. (1999). The chameleon effect: The perception-behavior link and social interaction. *Journal of Personality and Social Psychology*, 76 (6), 893–910.

Cheng, Y., Metzoff, A.M., & Decety, J. (2007). Motivation modulates the activity of the human mirror system: An fMRI study. *Cerebral cortex*, 17, 1979–1986.

Cherlunik, P.D., Donley, K.A., Wiewel, T.S.R., & Miller, S. R. (2001). Charisma is contagious: the effect of leaders' charisma on observers' affect. *Journal of Applied Social Psychology*, 31, 2149–59.

Chester, E. (2002). *Employing generation why? Understanding, managing, and motivating your new work force*, Lakewood, CO: Tucker House Books.

Cialdini, R. B., Brown, S. L., Lewis, B. P., Luce, C., & Neuberg, S. L. (1997). Reinterpreting the empathy altruism relationship: When one into one equals oneness. *Journal of Personality and Social Psychology*, 73, 481–494.

Clarke, N. (2008). Respect in Leadership: The Increasing Need for Empathy in Managers. (April 8, 2013). Available at http://www.ufhrd.co.uk/wordpress/wp-content/uploads/2008/06/608-respect-in-leadership-the-increasing-need-for-empathy-i.pdf.

Conway, N., & Briner, R. (2005). *Understanding psychological contracts at work: A critical evaluation of theory and research*. Oxford, UK: Oxford University Press.

Cozolino, L. (2006). *The neuroscience of human relationships: Attachment and the developing social brain*. New York: W.W. Norton.

Cozolino, L. (2010). *The neuroscience of psychotherapy: Healing the social brain* (2nd ed.). New York: Norton.

Craig, K. D. (2007). Assessment of credibility. In R. F. Schmidt & W. D. Willis (Eds.). *Encyclopedia of pain* (pp. 491–493). New York: Springer-Verlag.

Creswell, D. J., Way, B. M., Eisenberger, N. I., & Lieberman, M. D. (2007). Neural correlates of dispositional mindfulness during affect labeling. *Psychosomatic Medicine*, 69, 560–565.

Critchley, H. D. (2005). Neural mechanisms of autonomic, affective, and cognitive integration. *Comparative Neurology*, 493, 154–166.

Critchley, H. D., Wiens, S., Rothstein, P., Öhman, A., & Dolan, R. D. (2004). Neural systems supporting interoceptive awareness. *Nature Neuroscience*, 7, 189–195.

Dalgleish, T. (2004). The emotional brain. *Nature Reviews Neuroscience*, 5, pp. 583–589.

Damasio, A. (1994). *Descartes' error: Emotion, reason, and the human brain*. New York: Avon Books.

Damasio, A. (1999). *The feeling of what happens: Body and emotion in the making of consciousness*. San Diego, CA: Harvest.

Danziger, N., Prkachin, K., & Willer, J. (2006). Is pain the price of empathy? The perception of others' pain in patients with congenital sensitivity to pain. *Brain*, 129, 2494–2507.

Darwin, C. (1998). *The expression of the emotions in man and animals*, 3rd ed. New York: Oxford University Press.

Davidson, R. J. (1995). Cerebral assymetry, emotion, and affective style. In R. J. Davidson & L. Nadel (Eds.). *Brain assymetry* (pp. 361–387). New York: Oxford University Press.

Davidson, R. J., Jackson, D. C., & Kalin, N. H. (2000). Emotion, plasticity, context, and regulation: Perspectives from affective neuroscience. *Psychological Bulletin*, 126, 89–909.

Davidson, R. J., Kabat-Zinn, J., Schumacher, J., Rosenkranz, M., Muller, D., Santorelli, S. F., et al. (2003). Alterations in brain and immune function produced by mindfulness medication. *Psychosomatic Medicine*, 65(4), 564–570.

Davis, M. (2006). Neural systems involved in fear and anxiety measured with fear-potentiated startle. *American Psychologist*, 61, 741–756.

Davis, M. H. (1980). A multidimensional approach to the study of empathy. *JSAS Catalog of Selected Documents in Psychology*, 10, 85.

Davis, M. H. (1983). The effects of dispositional empathy on emotional reactions and helping: A multidimensional approach. *Journal of Personality*, 51, (2), 167–184.

Davis, M. H. (1983). Measuring individual differences in empathy: Evidence for a multidimensional approach. *Journal of Personality and Social Psychology*, 44, 113–236.

Davis, M. H. (1985). Perceptual and affective reverberation components. In A. B. Goldstein & G. Y. Michaels (Eds.). *Empathy: Development, training, and consequences* (pp. 62–108). Hillsdale, NJ: Erlbaum.

Davis, M. H. (1996). *Empathy: A social psychological approach*. Madison, WI: Westview Press.

Davis, M. H., Conklin, L., Smith, A., & Luce, C. (1996). Effect of perspective taking on the cognitive representation of persons: A merging of self and other. *Journal of Personality and Social Psychology*, 70, 713–726.

Davis, M. H., & Kraus, L. A. (1997). Personality and empathic accuracy. In W. Ickes (Eds.) *Empathic accuracy* (pp. 144–168). New York: Guilford Press.

de Waal, F. (1996). *Good natured: The origins of right and wrong in humans and animals*. Cambridge, MA: Harvard University Press.

De Vignemont, F., & Singer, T. (2006). Empathic brain: How, when and why? *Trends in Cognitive Sciences*, 10, 35–41.

Decety, J. (2005). Perspective taking as the royal avenue to empathy. In B. F. Malle and S. D. Hodges (Eds.), *Other minds: How humans bridge the divide between self and other* (pp. 135–149). New York: Guildford Press.

Decety, J. (2006). A cognitive neuroscience view of imitation. In S. Rogers & J. Williams (Eds.), *Imitation and the social mind: Autism and typical development* (pp. 251–274). New York: Guilford Press.

Decety, J., & Chaminade, T. (2005). The neurophysicology of imitation and intersubjectivity. In S. Hurley & N. Chater (Eds.), *Perspectives on imitation: From neuroscience to social science: Vol. 1. Mechanisms of imitation and imitation in animals* (pp. 119–140). Cambridge, MA: MIT Press.

Decety, J., & Grèzes, J. (2006). The power of simulation: Imagining one's own and other's behavior. *Brain Research*, 1079, 4–14.

Decety, J., & Hodges, S. D. (2006). A social cognitive neuroscience model of human empathy. In P. A. M. van Lange (Ed.), *Bridging social psychology: Benefits of trans disciplinary approaches* (pp. 103–109). Mahwah, NJ: Erlbaum.

Decety, J., & Jackson, P.L. (2004). The functional architecture of human empathy. *Behavioral and Cognitive Neuroscience Reviews*, 3, 71–100.

Decety, J., & Keenan, J. P. (2006). Social neuroscience: A new journal. *Social Neuroscience*, 1, 1–4.

Decety, J., & Lamm, C. (2006). Human empathy through the lens of social neuroscience. *Scientific World Journal* 6, 1146–1163.

Decety, J., & Lamm, C. (2007). The role of the right temporoparietal junction in social interaction: How low-level computational processes contribute to meta-cognition. *Neuroscientist*, 13, 580–593.

Decety, J., & Sommerville, J. A. (2003). Shared representations between self and others: A social cognitive neuroscience view. *Trends in Cognitive Sciences*, 7, 527–533.

Dennett, D. C. (1993). *Consciousness explained*. New York: Penguin.

Desimone, R., & Duncan, J. (1995). Neural mechanisms of selective visual attention. *Annual Review of Neuroscience*, 18, 193–222.

DeVignemont, F., & Singer, T. (2006). The empathic brain: How, when and why? *Trends in Cognitive Sciences*, 10 (10), 435–441.

Dijksterhuis, A. (2005). Why we are social animals: The high road to imitation as social glue. In S. Hurley & N. Chater (Eds.), *Perspectives on imitation: From cognitive neuroscience to social science: Vol. 2. Imitation, human development, and culture* (pp. 207–220). Cambridge, MA: MIT Press.

Dimberg, U. (1982). Facial reactions to facial expressions. *Psychophysiology*, 19,643–647.

Dobbs, D. (2006, April/May). Human see, human do. *Scientific American Mind*, 22–27.

Doherty, R. W. (1997). The emotional contagion scale: A measure of individual differences. *Journal of Nonverbal Behavior*, 21, 131–154.

Dolan R. J. (2007). The human amygdala and orbital prefrontal cortex in behavioral regulation. *Philos Trans R Soc Lond B Biol Sci*, 362, 787–99.

Domes, G., Heinrichs, M., Michel, A., Berger, C., & Herpertz, S. C. (2007). Oxytocin improves "mind-reading" in humans. *Biological Psychiatry*, 61, 731–733.

Drevets, W. C. (1999). Prefrontal cortical-amygdalar in metabolism major depression. *Annals of the New York Academy of Sciences*, 877, 614–637.

Drevets, W. C. (2003). Neuroimaging abnormalities in the amygdala in mood disorders. *Annals of New York Academy of Sciences*, 985, 420–444.

Ecker, B. (2008). Unlocking the emotional brain: Finding the neural key to transformation. *Psychotherapy Networker*, 32 (5), 42–47, 60.

Ecker, B. (2010). The brain's rules for change: Translating cutting-edge neuroscience into practice. *Psychotherapy Networker*, 34 (1), 43–45, 60.

Eichenbaum H. (2001). The hippocampus and declarative memory: cognitive mechanisms and neural codes. *Behav Brain Res*, 127, 199–207.

Eisenberg, N. (2000). Emotion, regulation, and moral development. *Annual Review of Psychology*, 51, 665–697.

Eisenberg, N. (2002). Distinctions among various modes of empathy-related reactions: A matter of importance to human relations. *Behavioral and Brain Sciences*, 25, 33–34.

Eisenberg, N., & Fabes, R. A. (1990). Empathy: Conceptualization, measurement, and relation to prosocial behavior. *Motivation and Emotion*, 14, 131–149.

Eisenberg, N., & Fabes, R. A. (1992). Emotion regulation and the development of social competence. In M. S. Clark (Ed.), *Review of personality and social psychology: Vol. 14. Emotion and social behavior* (pp. 119–150). Newbury Park, CA: Sage.

Eisenberg, N., Fabes, R. A., Murphy, B., Karbon, M., Maszk, P., Smith, M., O'Boyle, C., & Suh, K. (1994). The relations of emotionality and regulation to dispositional and situational empathy-related responding. *Journal of Personality and Social Psychology*, 66, 776–797.

Eisenberger, N. I., Lieberman, M. D., & Williams, K. D. (2003). Does rejection hurt? An fMRI study of social exclusion. *Science*, 10, 302, 290–292.

Eisenberg, N., & Miller, P. A. (1987). The relation of empathy to prosocial and related behaviors. *Psychological Bulletin*, 101 (1), 91–119.

Eisenberg, N., Shea, C. L., Carlo, G., & Knight, G. P. (1991). Empathy-related responding and cognition: A "chicken and the egg" dilemma. In W. M. Kurtines (Ed.), *Handbook of moral behavior and development: Vol. 2. Research* (pp. 63–88). Hillsdale, NJ: Erlbaum.

Eisenberg, N., & Strayer, J. (Eds.). (1987). *Empathy and its development.* New York: Cambridge University Press.

Eisenberg, N., Valiente, C., & Champion, C. (2004). Empathy-related responding: Moral, social, and socialization correlates. In A. G. Miller (Ed.), *The social psychology of good and evil: Understanding our capacity for kindness and cruelty* (pp. 386–415). New York: Guilford Press.

Ekman, P., & Friesen, W. V. (1975). *Unmasking the face: A guide to recognizing emotions from facial expressions.* Englewood Cliffs, NJ: Prentice-Hall.

Elliott, R., Watson, J., Goldman, R., & Greenberg, L. S. (2004). *Learning emotion-focused therapy: The process-experiential approach to change.* Washington, DC: American Psychological Association.

"Empathetic Leadership." Safety-related leadership throughout a work culture (April 8, 2013). Available at http://www.safetyperformance.com/EmpathicLeadership.pdf.

"Empathy: A Clinician's Perspective." The ASHA Leader (April 8, 2013). Available at www.asha.org/Publications/leader/2006/060815/f060815e.htm.

"Empathy in business: indulgence or invaluable?" Forbes (April 8, 2013). Available at http://www.forbes.com/sites/ashoka/2013/03/22/empathy-in-business-indulgence-or-invaluable/.

"Empathy in Communication" Selfgrowth.com (April 8, 2013). Available at www.selfgrowth.com/articles/winnett2.html.

"Empathy in Leadership--10 Reasons Why It Matters" Tanveernaseer.com. June 2011blog (April 8, 2013). Available at http://www.tanveernaseer.com/why-empathy-matters-in-leadership/.

"Empathy in the Workplace: Tools for Effective Leadership, A White Paper" Center for Creative Leadership (April 8, 2013). Available at http://www.ccl.org/leadership/pdf/research/EmpathyInTheWorkplace.pdf.

"Empathy: leadership strength or weakness?" Positive Business DC (April 8, 2013). Available at http://positivebusinessdc.com/empathy-leadership-strength-or-weakness/.

"Empathy, trust, diffusing conflict & handling complaints." Businessballs.com (April 8, 2013). Available at www.businessballs.com/empathy.htm.

Eppert, F., et al. (2007). Regulation of emotional responses elicited by threat-related stimuli. *Hum Brain Mapp.* 28:409–23.

Erez, A., & Isen, A.M. (2002). The influence of positive affect on the components of expectancy motivation. *Journal of Applied Psychology*, 87, 1055–1067.

Eslinger, P.J. (1998). Neurological and neuropsychological bases of empathy. *European Neurology*, 39, 1998, 193–199.

Fadiga, L., Craighero, L., & Olivier, E. (2005). Human motor cortex excitability during the perception of others' actions. *Current Opinion in Neurobiology*, 15, 213–218.

Farb, N. A. S., Segal, Z. V., Mayberg, H., Bean, J., McKeon, D., & Fatima, Z. (2007). Attending to the present: Mindfulness meditation reveals distinct neural modes of self-reference. *Social Cognitive and Affective Neuroscience*, 2, 313–322.

Fellows, L. K., & Farah, M. J. (2007). The role of the ventromedial prefrontal cortex in decision making: Judgment under uncertainty or judgment per se? *Cerebral Cortex*, 17 (11), 2669–2674. doi:10.1093/cercor/bhl176.

Ferrari, P. F., Gallese, V., Rizzolatti, G., & Fogassi, L. (2003). Mirror neurons responding to the observation of ingestive and communicative mouth actions in the monkey premotor cortex. *European Journal of Neuroscience*, 17, 1703–1714.

Feshbach, N. D., Feshbach, S., Fauvre, M., & Ballard-Campbell, M. (1984). *Learning to care: A curriculum for affective and social development*. Glenview, IL: Scott, Foresman.

Finger, E. C., Marsh, A. A., Kamel, N., Mitchell, D. G., & Blair, J. R. (2006). Caught in the act: The impact of audience on the neural response to morally and socially inappropriate behavior. *NeuroImage*, 33 (1), 414–421.

Fiske, S. T. (1993). Controlling other people: The impact of power on stereotyping. *American Psychologist*, 48, 621–628.

Fitzgerald, D. A., Angstadt, M., Jelsone, L. M., Nathan, P. J., & Phan, K. L. (2006). Beyond threat: Amygdala reactivity across multiple expressions of facial affect. *NeuroImage*, 30 (4), 1441–1448.

Floyd, J. F. (1985). *Listening: A practical approach*. London: Scott, Foresman.

Forgas, J.P., & George, J.M. (2001). Affective influences on judgments and behavior in organizations: An information processing perspective. *Organizational Behavior and Human Decision Processes*, 86, pp. 3–34.

Forgas, J.P. (1995). Mood and judgment: The affective infusion model (AIM). *Psychological Bulletin*, 117, pp. 39–66.

Fosha, D. (2001). The dyadic regulation of affect. *Journal of Clinical Psychology*, 57, 227–242.

Fosha, D., Siegel, D. J., & Solomon, M.F. (Eds.). (2009). *The healing power of emotion: Affective neuroscience, development, and clinical practice*. New York: Norton.

Fox, D. (2008, November 5). The Secret life of the brain. *NewScientist Magazine*, 2681, 30–33.

Frith, C. D., & Frith, U. (2006). The neural basis of metalizing. *Neuron*, 50 (4), 531–534.

Frodl, T., Meisenzahl, E., Zetzsche, T., Bottlender, R., Born, C., Groll, C., et al. (2002). Enlargement of the amygdala in patients with a first episode of major depression. *Biological Psychology*, 51(9), 708–714.

Fuster, J. M. (1997). *The prefrontal cortex*. Philadelphia: Lippincott, Raven.

Gallese, V. (2005). "Being like me": Self-other identity, mirror neurons, and empathy. In S. Hurley & N. Chater (Eds.), *Perspectives on imitation: From neuroscience to social science: Vol. 1. Mechanisms of imitation and imitation in animals* (pp. 101–118). Cambridge, MA: MIT Press.

Gallese, V. (2006). Intentional attunement: A neurophysiological perspective on social cognition and its disruption in autism. *Brain Research*, 1079 (1), 15–24.

Gallese, V., Fadiga, L., Fogassi, L., & Rizzolatti, G. (1996). Action recognition in the premotor cortex. *Brain*, 119, 595–609.

Gallese, V., Ferrari, P.F., & Umilta, M.A. (2002). The mirror matching system: A shared manifold for intersubjectivity. *Behavioral and Brain Sciences*, 25, 35–36.

Gallese, V., & Goldman, A. (1998). Mirror neurons and the simulation theory of mind-readying. *Trends in Cognitive Sciences*, 2 (12), 493–501.

Gallese, V., Keysers, C., & Rizzolatti, G. (2004). A unifying view of the basis of social cognition. *Trends in Cognitive Sciences*, 8 (9), 396–403.

Gallup, G. G., Jr. (1982). Self-awareness and the emergence of mind in primates. *American Journal of Primatology*, 2 (3), 237–248.

Gazzaniga, M. S., Ivry, R. B., & Mangun, G. R. (2002). *Cognitive neuroscience: The biology of the mind*. New York: Norton.

Gazzola, V., Aziz-Zadeh, L., & Keysers, C. (2006). Empathy and the somatotopic auditory mirror system in humans. *Current Biology*, 16, 1824–1829.

Gergely, G., & Watson, J. (2002). The social bio-feedback model of parental affect-mirroring. In P. Fonagy, G. Gergely, E. L. Jurist, & M. Target (Eds.), *Affect regulation, mentalization and the development of the self* (pp. 145–202). New York: Other Press.

Germer, C., & Salzberg, S. (2009). *The mindful path to self-compassion: Freeing yourself from destructive thoughts and emotions*. New York: Guilford Press.

Ginot, E. (2009). The empathic power of enactments: The link between neuropsychosocial processes and an expanded definition of empathy. *Psychoanalytic Psychology*, 26(3), 290–309. Doi:10.3037/a0016449.

Gist, M. E., & Mitchell, T. E. (1992). Self-efficacy: A theoretical analysis of its determinants and malleability. *Academy of Management Review*, 17, 183–211.

Goel, V., Grafman, J., Sadato, N., & Hallett, M. (1995). Modeling other minds. *Neuroreport*, 6, 1741–1746.

Goffman, E. (1974). *Frame analysis: An essay on the organization of experience*. New York: Harper Colophon.

Goldie, P. (1999). How we think of others' emotions. *Mind and Language*, 14 (4), 394–423.

Goldman, A. I. (2006). *Simulating minds: The philosophy, psychology, and neuroscience of mindreading*. New York: Oxford University Press.

Goldman-Rakic, P. S. (1995). Toward a circuit model of working memory and the guidance of voluntary motor action. In J. C. Houk, J. L. Davis, D. G. Beiser, (Eds.), *Models of Information Processing in the Basal Ganglia* (pp. 131–48). Boston, MA: MIT Press, 1995.

Goldstein, A. P. & Michaels, G.Y. (1985). *Empathy: Development, training and consequences*. London: Lawrence Erlbaum Associates.

Goleman, D. (2006). *Social intelligence: The new science of human relationships*. New York: Bantam.

Gompertz, K. (1960). The relation of empathy to effective communication. *Journalism Quarterly*, 17, 533–546.

Goubert, L., Craig, K. D., Vervoort, T., Morley, S., Sullivan, M. J. L., Williams, A. C. de C., Cano, A., & Crombez, G. (2005). Facing others in pain: The effects of empathy. *Pain*, 118, 285–288.

Gould, E., Reeves, A. J., Graziano, M. S. A., & Gross, C. G. (1999). Neurogenesis in the neocortex of adult primates. *Science*, 286, 548–552.

Grattan, L. M., Bloomer, R. H., Archambault, F. X., & Eslinger, P. J. (1994). Cognitive flexibility and empathy after frontal lobe lesion. *Neuropsychiatry, Neuropsychology, and Behavioral Neurology*, 7, 251–257.

Green, J. D., Sommerville, R. B., Nystron, L. E., Darley, J. M., & Cohen, J. D. (2001). An fMRI investigation of emotional engagement in moral judgment. *Science*, 293, 1971–1972.

Greenberg, J. (1987). A taxonomy of organizational justice theories. *Academy of Management Review*, 12, pp. 9–22.

Greenberg, L. S., Rice, L. N., & Elliott, R. (1993). *Facilitating emotional change: The moment-by-moment process*. New York: Guilford Press.

Greenberg, L. S., & Rushanski-Rosenberg, R. (2002). Therapist's experience of empathy. In J. C. Watson, R. N. Goldman, & M. S. Warner (Eds.), *Client-centered and experiential psychotherapy in the 21st century: Advances in theory, research and practice* (168–181). Ross-on Wye, UK: PCCS Books.

Griffin, R. (2012). *Fundamentals of Management* (6th Edition). Mason, OH: South-Western.

Grippo, A. J., Gerena, D., Huang, J., Kumar, N., Shah, M., Ughreja, R., & Carter, C. S. (2007). Social isolation induces behavioral and neuroendocrine disturbances relevant to depression in female and male prairie voles. *Psychoneuroendocrinology*, 32, 966–980.

Grippo, A. J., Lamb, D. G., Carter, C. S., & Porges, S. W. (2007). Cardiac regulation in the socially monogamous prairie vole. *Physiology and Behavior*, 90, 386–393.

Grosbras, M. H., & Paus, T. (2006). Brain networks involved in viewing angry hands or faces. *Cerebral Cortex*, 16, 1087–1096.

Gross, J.J., & John, O. P. (2003). Individual differences in two emotion regulation processes: Implications for affect, relationships, and well-being. *Journal of Personality and Social Psychology*, 85, 348–362.

Gurvits, T., Shenton, M., Hokama, H., Ohta, H., Lasko, N., Gilbertson, M., et al. (1996). Magnetic resonance imaging study of hippocampal volume in chronic, combat-related posttraumatic stress disorder. *Biological Psychiatry*, 40, 1091–1099.

Haidt, J. (2000). The emotional dog and its rational tail: A social intuitionist approach to moral judgment. *Psychological Review*, 108, pp. 814–834.

Håkansson, Jakob (2003). "Exploring the Phenomenon of Empathy." Doctoral dissertation in the Dept. of Psychology at Stockholm University (April 8, 2013). Available at www.communicationcache.com/uploads/1/0/8/8/10887248/exploring_the_phenomenon_of_empathy.pdf.

Halgren, E. (1992). Emotional neurophysiology of the amygdala within the context of human cognition. In J. P. Aggleton (Ed.), *The amygdala: Neurobiological aspects of emotion, memory, and mental dysfunction* (pp. 191–228). New York: Wiley-Liss.

Hall, D. A., Morgeson, F. P., & Bernieri, F. J. (Eds.), (2001). *Interpersonal sensitivity: Theory and measurement*. Hillsdale, NJ: Erlbaum.

Hamilton, A. F., & Grafton, S. T. (2006). Goal representation in human anterior intraparietal sulcus. *Journal of Neuroscience*, 26, (4), 1133–1137.

Hancock, J., Landrigan, C., & Silver, C. (April 2007). "Expressing emotion in text-based communication," Online edition of CHI Proceedings: Emotion & Empathy. Available at http://nguyendangbinh.org/Proceedings/CHI/2007/docs/p929.pdf.

Harbach, R. L., & Asbury, F. R. (1976). Some effects of empathic understanding on negative student behaviors. *Humanist Educator*, 15, 19–24.

Hare, R. D. (1991). *The hare psychopathy checklist – Revised*. Toronto: Multi-Health Systems.

Harpur, T. J., & Hare, R. D. (1994). Assessment of psychopathy as a function of age. *Journal of Abnormal Psychology*, 103, 604–609.

Harris, J. C. (2003). Social neuroscience, empathy, brain integration, and neurodevelopmental disorders. *Physiology and Behavior*, 79, 525–531.

Harris, J. C. (2007). The evolutionary neurobiology, emergence and facilitation of empathy. In T. F. D. Farrow & P. W. R. Woodruff, *Empathy in mental illness*. New York: Cambridge University Press.

Hatfield, E., Cacioppo, J., & Rapson, R. (1994). *Emotional contagion*. Cambridge: Cambridge University Press.

Hatfield, E., Hsee, C.K., Costello, J., Weisman, M.S., & Denney, C. (1995). The impact of vocal feedback on emotional experience and expression. *Journal of Social Behavior and Personality*, 10, 293–312.

Hauser, M. D. (2000). *Wild minds: What animals really think*. New York: Holt.

Herzberg, F.I. (1987). "One more time: How do you motivate employees?" *Harvard Business Review*, 65(5), 109–120.

Hickson, M. III, & Neiva, E. (2002). Toward a taxonomy of universals in the biology of communication. *Journal of Intercultural Communication Research*, 31, 149–166.

Hickson, M. III, & Neiva, E. (2003). Communication, biology, and culture. *Journal of Intercultural Communication Research*, 32, 1–8.

Hickson, M. III, Powell, L., Turner, J., Neiva, E., & Adams, C. T. (2002). The somatic marker as a "short cut" to verbal immediacy. *Communication Research Reports*, 19, 389–398.

Hodges, S. D., & Klein, K. J. K. (2001). Regulating the costs of empathy: The price of being human. *Journal of Socio-Economics*, 30, 437–452.

Hodges, S. D., & Wegner, D. M. (1997). Automatic and controlled empathy. In W. Ickes (Ed.), *Empathic accuracy* (pp. 311–339). New York: Guilford Press.

Hoffman, M. (2000). *Empathy and moral development: Implications for caring and justice*. New York: Cambridge University Press.

Hoffman, M. L. (1970). Conscience, personality and socialization techniques. *Human Development*, 13, 90–126.

Hoffman, M. L. (1983). Affective and cognitive processes in moral internalization. In E. T. Higgins, D. N. Rubel, & W. W. Hartup (Eds.), *Social Cognition and Social Development: A Socio-Cultural Perspective* (pp. 236–274). Cambridge: Cambridge University Press.

Hogan, K., & Stubbs, R. (2003). *Can't get through 8 barriers to communication.* Grenta, LA: Pelican Publishing Company.

Homans, G. C. (1974). *Social behavior: Its elementary forms.* Rev. ed. New York: Harcourt, Brace, and Jovanovich.

House, R.J., & Podsakoff, P.M. (1994). Leadership effectiveness: Past perspectives and future directions for research. In J. Greenberg (Ed.) *Organizational behavior: the state of the science* (pp 45–82). Hillsdale. NJ: Lawrence Erlbaum Associates.

"How to Develop Empathy in Business Communication." Houston Chronicle online (April 8, 2013). Available at http://smallbusiness.chron.com/develop-empathy-business-communication-30895.html.

Hurley, S., & Chater, N. (2005). *Perspectives on imitation: From neuroscience to social science: Vol. 1. Mechanisms of imitation and imitation in animals.* Cambridge, MA: MIT Press.

Hurley, S., & Chater, N. (2005). *Perspectives on imitation: From neuroscience to social science: Vol. 2. Imitation, human development, and culture.* Cambridge, MA: MIT Press.

Huttenlocher, P. R. (2002). *Neural plasticity: The effects of environment on the development of the cerebral cortex.* Cambridge, MA: Harvard University Press.

Iacoboni, M. (2005). Understanding others: Imitation, language, and empathy. In S. Hurley & N. Chater (Eds.), *Perspectives on imitation: From neuroscience to social science: Vol. 1. Mechanisms of imitation and imitation in animals* (pp.77–99). Cambridge, MA: MIT Press.

Iacoboni, M. (2007). Face to face: The neural basis of social mirroring and empathy. *Psychiatric Annals,* 374, 236–241.

Iacoboni, M. (2009). Imitation, empathy, and mirror neurons. *Annual Review of Psychology,* 60, 653–670.

Iacoboni, M., & Badenoch, B. (2010, Spring). Discovering our brain's many mirrors. Connections and Reflections: *The GAINS Quarterly,* 3–9.

Iacoboni, M., & Dapretto, M. (2006). The mirror neuron system and the consequences of its dysfunction. *Nature Reviews Neuroscience,* 7, 942–951.

Iacoboni, M., Molnar-Szakacs, I., Gallese, V., Buccino, G., Mazziotta, J. C., & Rizzolatti, G. (2005). "Grasping the intentions of others with one's own mirror neuron system." *Public Library of Science Biology*, no. 3, 529–535.

Iacoboni, M., Woods, R. P., Brass, M., Bekkering, H., Mazziotta, J. C., & Rizzolatti, G. (1999). Cortical mechanisms of human imitation. *Science*, 286 (5449), 2526–2528.

Ickes, W. (2001). Measuring empathic accuracy. In J. A. Hall, F. J. Hall, & F. J. Bernieri (Eds.), *Interpersonal sensitivity: Theory and measurement* (pp. 291–241). Mahwah, NJ: Erlbaum.

Ickes, W. (2003). *Everyday mind reading: Understanding what other people think and feel*. Amherst, NY: Prometheus Books.

Ickes, W., C. Marangoni, and S. Garcia. (1997). Studying empathic accuracy in a clinically relevant context, in *Empathic Accuracy*, pp. 282–310.

Ickes, W., & Simpson, J. A. (2001). Motivational aspects of empathic accuracy. In G. J. O. Fletcher & M. S. Clark (Eds), *Interpersonal processes: Blackwell handbook in social psychology* (pp. 229–249). Oxford: Blackwell.

Isen, A. M. (2000). Positive affect and decision making. In M. Lewis & J. M. Haviland-Jones (Eds.), *Handbook of emotions* (2nd ed.), (pp. 417–435). New York: Guilford Press.

Izard, C.E. (1993). Four systems for emotion activation: Cognitive and non-cognitive processes. *Psychological Review*, 100, pp. 60–69.

Jackson, P.L., Brunet, E., Meltzoff, A. N., & Decety, J. (2006). Empathy examined through the neural mechanisms involved in imagining how I feel versus how you feel in pain. *Neuropsychologia*, 44, 752–761.

Jackson, P. L., Meltzoff, A. N., & Decety, J. (2005). How do we perceive the pain of others? A window into the neural processes involved in empathy. *NeuroImage*, 24 (3), 771–779.

Jackson, P. L., Rainville, P., & Decety, J. (2006). To what extent do we share the pain of others? Insight from the neural bases of pain empathy. *Pain*, 125, 5–9.

Johnson, M. (1987). *The body in the mind: The bodily basis of meaning, imagination, and reason*. Chicago: University of Chicago Press.

Joseph R. (1998). Traumatic amnesia, repression, and hippocampus injury due to emotional stress, corticosteroids and enkeptalins. *Child Psychiatry Hum Dev*. 29:169–85.

Kabat-Zinn, J. (2003). *Coming to our senses: Healing ourselves and the world through mindfulness.* New York: Hyperion Press.

Kabat-Zinn, J. (2005). *Wherever you go, there you are: Mindfulness meditation in everyday life.* New York: Hyperion.

Kagan, J., & Lamb, S. (1987). *The emergence of morality in your children.* Chicago: University of Chicago Press.

Kaplan, J. T., & Iacoboni, M. (2006). Getting a grip on other minds: Mirror neurons, intention understanding and cognitive empathy. *Social Neuroscience, 1*, 175–183.

Katz, R. L. (1963). *Empathy: Its nature and uses.* New York: Free Press.

Kellett, J.B., Humphrey, R. H., & Sleeth, R. G. (2002). Empathy and complex task performance. *The Leadership Quarterly*, 523–544.

Kendler, K. S., Kuhn, J. W., Vittum, J., Prescott, C. A., & Riley, B. (2005). The interaction of stressful life events and a serotonin transporter polymorphism in the prediction of episodes of major depression: A replication. *Archives of General Psychiatry, 62*, 529–535.

Kennedy-Moore, E., & Watson, J. C. (1999). *Expressing emotion: Myths, realities and therapeutic strategies.* New York: Guilford Press.

Kerns, J. G., Cohen, J. D., MacDonall, A. W., Cho, R. Y., Stenger, V.A., & Carter, C. S. (2004). Anterior cingulate conflict monitoring and adjustments in control. *Science, 303*, 1023–1026.

Keysers, C., & Gazzola, V. (2007). Integrating simulation and theory of mind: From self to social cognition. *Trends in Cognitive Sciences, 11*, 194–196.

Kiehl, K. A., Smith, A. M., Hare, R. D., Mendrek, A., Forster, B. B., Brink, Jr., & Liddle, P. F. (2001). Limbic abnormalities in affective processing by criminal psychopaths as revealed by functional magnetic resonance imaging. *Biological Psychiatry, 50*, 677–684.

Kinsbourne, M. (2002). The role of imitation in body ownership and mental growth. In A. N. Metzoff & W. Prinz (Eds.), *The imitative mind: Development, evolution, and brain bases* (pp.311–330). New York: Cambridge University Press.

Kirsch, P., Esslinger, C., Chen, Q., Mier, D., Lis, S., Siddhanti, S., Gruppe, H., Mattay, V. S., Gallhofer, B., & Meyer-Lindenberg, A. (2005). Oxytocin modulates neural circuitry for social cognition and fear in humans. *Journal of neuroscience, 25*, 11489–11493.

Kohn, A. (1990). *The brighter side of human nature: Altruism and empathy in everyday life.* New York: Basic Books, Inc.

Kohn, A. (1993). *Punished by rewards: The trouble with gold stars, incentive plans, A's, praise, and other bribes,* New York: Houghton Mifflin.

Kosfeld, M., Heinrichs, M., Zak, P. J., Fischbacher, U., & Fehr, E. (2005). Oxytocin increases trust in humans. *Nature, 435,* 673–676.

Krebs, D. 1975. "Empathy and altruism." *Journal of Personality and Social Psychology 32,* 1134–46.

Kremer, J. F., & Dietzen, L. L. (1991). Two approaches to teaching accurate empathy in undergraduates: Teacher intensive and self-directed. *Journal of College Student Development, 32,* 69–75.

LaBar, K., & LeDoux, J. E. (1996). *Emotion and the brain: An overview.* In T. Feinberg & M. Farah (Eds.), *Behavioral neurology and neuropsychology.* New York: Academic.

LaFrance, M. (1982). Posture mirroring and rapport. In M. Davis (Ed.), *Interaction rhythms: Periodicity in communicative behavior* (pp. 279–298). New York: Human Sciences Press.

Lambert, M. J., & Ogles, B. M. (2004). The efficacy and effectiveness of psychotherapy. In M. J. Lambert (Ed.) *Bergin and Garfield's handbook of psychotherapy and behavior change* (5th ed., pp. 139–193). New York: Wiley.

Lamm, C., Batson, C., & Decety, J. (2007). The neural substrate of human empathy: Effects of perspective-taking and cognitive appraisal. *Journal of Cognitive Neuroscience, 19,* 42–58.

Langford, D. J., Crager, S. E., Shehzad, Z., Smith, S. B., Sotocinal, S. G., Levendstad, J. S., Chanda, M. L., Levitin, D. J., & Mogil, J. S. (2006). Social modulation of pain as evidence for empathy in mice. *Science, 312,* 1967–1970.

Lanzetta, J. T., & Englis, B. G. (1989). Expectations of cooperation and competition and their effect on observers' vicarious emotional responses. *Journal of Personality and Social Psychology, 56,* 543–554.

Larson C. L., et al. (2006). Fear is fast in phobic individuals; amygdala activation in response to fear-relevant stimuli. *Biol Psychiatry 60,* 410–7.

Lasher, Margot (1992). *The art and practice of compassion and empathy.* New York: Tarcher/Perigee Books.

Lawrence, E. J., Shaw P., Giampietro, V. P., Surgulaze, S., Brammer, M. J., & David, A. S. (2006). The role of "shared representations" in social perception and empathy: An fMRI study. *NeuroImage*, 29 (4), 1173–1184.

"Leadership character: The role of empathy; part 4 of a 6 part leadership series" The Washington Post (April 8, 2013). Available at http://www.washingtonpost.com/blogs/guest-insights/post/leadership-character-the-role-of-empathy/2011/04/04/gIQAQXVGQM_blog.html.

LeDoux, J. (1986). Neurobiology of emotion. In J. E. LeDoux, W. Hirst (Eds.), *Mind and Brain: Dialogues in Cognitive Neuroscience*. New York: Cambridge University Press.

LeDoux, J. (1990). Fear Pathways in the Brain: Implications for Theories of the Emotional Brain. In P. Brain, S. Parmigiani, D. Maindardi, R. J. Blanchard (Eds.) *Fear and defense*. (London: Gordon and Breach).

LeDoux, J. (1991). Emotion and the limbic system concept. *Concepts Neurosci* 2:169–199.

LeDoux, J. (1992). Brain systems and emotional memory. In K. Strongman (Ed.), *International Review on Studies of Emotion*, pp 23–29. John Wiley.

LeDoux, J. (1992). Emotion and the amygdala. In J. Aggleton (Ed.), *The Amygdala*, pp 339–351. New York: Academic Press.

LeDoux, J. (1992). Emotional networks in the brain. In M. Lewis, & J. Haviland (Eds.), *Handbook of emotions*, pp. 109–118. New York: Guilford.

LeDoux, J. (1992). Emotional short-circuits in the brain. In B. Smith, G. Adelman (Eds.), *Neuroscience year: Supplement 2 to the encyclopedia of neuroscience*, pp 61–62. Boston: Birkhauser.

LeDoux, J. (1994). The amygdala: contributions to fear and stress. *Seminars in Neuroscience* 6, 231–237.

LeDoux, J. (1994). Emotion, memory and the brain. *Scientific American*, 270 (6), 50–57.

LeDoux, J. (1996). *The emotional brain: The mysterious underpinnings of emotional life*. New York: Simon and Schuster.

LeDoux, J. (1998). *The emotional brain*. New York: Weidenfeld & Nicolson.

LeDoux, J. (2000). The amygdala and emotion: A view through fear. In J.P. Aggleton (Ed.), *The amygdala: A functional analysis* (pp. 289–31). Oxford: Oxford University Press.

LeDoux J. (2000). Emotion circuits in the brain. *Annu. Rev. Neurosci.* 23, 155–84.

LeDoux, J. (2002). *Synaptic self: How our brains become who we are.* New York: Viking.

LeDoux, J. (2012). Rethinking the emotional brain. *Neuron* 73, 653–676.

Leslie, A. (1987). Pretense and representation: The origins of a "theory of mind." *Psychological Review*, 94, 412–426.

Leslie, K. R., Johnson-Frey, S. H., & Grafton, S. T. (2004). Functional imaging of face and hand imitation: Towards a motor theory of empathy. *NeuroImage*, 21 (2), 601–607.

Levenson, R. W., & Ruef, A. M. (1992). Empathy: A physiological substrate. *Journal of Personality and Social Psychology*, 63, 234–246.

Lewis, M., Sullivan, M. W., Stanger, C., & Weiss, M. (1989). Self-development and self-conscious emotion. *Child Development*, 60 (1), 146–156.

Lewis, T., M.D.,'s YouTube presentation for Google Corporation on neuroscience & empathy. (April 8, 2013). Available at http://www.youtube.com/watch?v=1-T2GsG0l1E.

Lipps, T. (1907). Das wissen von fremden Ichen. *Psychologischen Untersuchungen*, 1, 694–722.

Lipps, T. (1903). Einfuhlung, inner Nachahmung, und Organ-umpfindungen (Empathy, inner imitations, and sensations). *Archiv fur die gesamte Psycholgies*, 2, 185–204.

Lizarraga, L. S., Ugarte, M. D., Cardella-Elawar, M., Iriarte, M. D., & Baquedano, M. T. S. (2003). Enhancement of self-regulation, assertiveness, and empathy. *Learning and Instruction*, 13, (4), 423–439.

Loewenstein, G.F., Weber, E.U., Hsee, C.K., and Welch, N. (2001). "Risk as Feelings." *Psychological Bulletin*, 127, pp. 267–286.

Lovett, B., & Sheffield, R. (2007). Affective empathy deficits in aggressive children and adolescents: A critical review. *Clinical Psychology Review*, 27, 1–13.

Luo, Q., Holroyd, T., Jones, M., Hendler, T., & Blair, J. (2007). Neural dynamics for facial threat processing as revealed by gamma band synchronization using MEG. *NeuroImage*, 34, (2), 839–847.

Luo, Q., Nakic, M., Wheatley, T., Richell, R., Martin, A., & Blair, R. J. (2006). The neural basis of implicit moral attitude: An IAT study using event-related fMRI. *NeuroImage*, 30 (4), 1449–1457.

Maak, T. & Pless, N.M. (2006). Responsible leadership in a stakeholder society – A relational perspective. *Journal of Business Ethics*, 66, 99–115.

Machado, P. P., Beutler, L. E., & Greenberg, L. S. (1999). Emotion recognition in psychotherapy: Impact of therapist level of experience and emotional awareness. *Journal of Clinical Psychology*, 55, 39–57.

MacLean, P. D. (1990). *The triune brain in evolution: Role in paleocerebral functions*. New York: Plenum Press.

Maguire, E. A., Gadian, D. G., Johnsrude, I. S., Good, C. D., Ashburner, J., Frackowiak, S. J., & Frith, C. D. (2000). Navigation-related structural change in the hippocampi of taxi drivers. *Proceedings of the National Academy of Science*, 97, 4398–4403.

Main, M. (1996). Introduction to the special section on attachment and psychopathology: 2. Overview of the field of attachment. *Journal of Consulting and Clinical Psychology*, 64, 237–243.

Main, M. (2000). The adult attachment interview: Fear, attention, safety, and discourse processes. *Journal of the American Psychoanalytic Association*, 48, 1055–1096.

Malcolm, N. (1963). Knowledge of other minds. In N. Malcolm, *Knowledge and certainty: Essays and lectures* (pp. 130–140). Englewood Cliffs, NJ: Prentice-Hall.

Marci, C. D., Ham, J., Moran, E. K., & Orr, S. P. (2007). Physiologic concordance, empathy, and social-emotional processing during psychotherapy. *Journal of Nervous and Mental Disease*, 195, 103–111.

Marci, C. D., & Reiss, H. (2005). The clinical relevance of psychophysiology: Support for the psychobiology of empathy and psychodynamic process. *American Journal of Psychotherapy*, 259, 213–226.

Marciano, P. (2010). *Carrots and Sticks Don't Work: Build a Culture of Employee Engagement with the Principles of RESPECT*, New York: McGraw-Hill.

Marsh, A. A., Adams, R. B., & Kleck, R. E. (2005). Why do fear and anger look the way they do? Form and social function in facial expressions. *Personality and Social Psychology Bulletin*, 31, 1–14.

Martinuzzi, B. (2009). *The leader as a mensch: Become the kind of person others want to follow*. San Francisco, CA: Six Seconds Emotional Intelligence Press.

Maslow, A. H. (1954). *Motivation and Personality*. New York: Harper & Row.

Maurer, R., & Tindall, J. (1983). Effect of postural congruence on client's perception of counselor empathy. *Journal of Counseling Psychology*, 30, 158–163.

Mayo, E. (1933). *The human problems of an industrialized civilization.* Chicago IL: Scott, Foresman.

McClelland, D. (1965). Achievement motivation can be developed. *Harvard Business Review*, 43, pp. 6–24.

McGaugh, J. L., Cahill, L., & Roozendaal, B. (1996). Involvement of the amygdala in memory storage: Interaction with other brain systems. *Proc Natl Acad Sci USA* 93, 13508–14.

McGaugh, J. L., & Gold, P.E. (1976). In M. R. Rosenzweig, & E. L. Bennett (Eds.), *Neural mechanisms of learning and memory* (pp 549–60). Cambridge, MA: MIT Press.

McGregor, D. M. (1960). *The human side of enterprise.* New York: McGraw-Hill.

McGregor, D. M. (1957). The human side of the enterprise. *Management Review*, 46, pp. 22–28.

McHugh, P. (1968). *Defining the situation: The organization of meaning in social interaction.* Indianapolis, IN: Bobbs-Merrill.

Mead, G. H. (1938). *The philosophy of the act.* Chicago: University of Chicago Press.

Mead, G. H. (1934). *Mind, self, and society: From the standpoint of a social behaviorist.* Chicago: University of Chicago Press.

Mehrabian, A., & Epstein, N. (1972). A measure of emotional empathy. *Journal of Personality*, 40 (4), 525–543.

Meltzoff, A. N., & Decety, J. (2003). What imitation tells us about social cognition: A rapprochement between developmental psychology and cognitive neuroscience. *Philosophical Transactions of the Royal Society*, London, B, 358, 491–500.

Meltzoff, A. N., & Moore, M. K. (1977). Imitation of facial and manual gestures by human neonates. *Science*, 198, 74–78.

Meltzoff, A. N., & Moore, M. K. (1994). Imitation, memory, and the representation of persons. *Infant Behavior and Development*, 17 (1), 83–99.

Miller, P. A., & Eisenberg, N. (1988). The relation of empathy to aggressive and externalizing/antisocial behavior. *Psychological Bulletin*, 103 (3), 324–344.

Mineka, S., & Cook, M. (1993). Mechanisms involved in the observational conditioning of fear. *Journal of Experimental Psychology: General*, 122, 23–38.

Mitchell, J. P., Banaji, M. R., & Macrae, C. N. (2005). The link between social cognition and self-referential thought in the medial prefrontal cortex. *Journal of Cognitive Neuroscience*, 17, 1306–1315.

Miyashiro, M. (2011). *The empathy factor: Your competitive advantage for personal, team, and business success.* Encinitas, CA: Puddle Dancer Press.

Moriguchi, Y., Decety, J., Ohnishi, T., Maeda, M., T., Nemoto, K., Matsuda, H., & Komaki, G. (2007). Empathy and judging other's pain: An fMFI study of alexithymia. *Cerebral Cortex*, 17, 2223–2234.

Morrison, I., Lloyd, D., di Pellegrino, G., & Roverts, N. (2004). Vicarious responses to pain in anterior cingulate cortex: Is empathy a multisensory issue? *Cognitive, Affective, and Behavioral Neuroscience*, 4(2), 270–278.

Muchinsky, P.M. (2000). Emotions in the workplace: The neglect of organizational behavior. *Journal of Organizational Behavior*, 21, pp. 801–805.

Myeong-Gu S., Feldman-Barrett, L., and Bartunek, J. (2004). The role of affective experience in work motivation. *Academy Management Review*, 29(3), pp. 423–439.

Nauta, Walle. (1971). The problem of the frontal lobe: A reinterpretation. *Journal of Psychiatric Research*, 8, 167–187.

Neiva, E., & Hickson, M. III (2003). Deception and honesty in animal and human communication: A new look at communicative interaction. *Journal of Intercultural Communication Research*, 32, 23–45.

Neubauer, P. B., & Neubauer, A. (1990). *Nature's thumbprint: The new genes of personality.* Reading, MA: Addison-Wesley.

Niedenthal, P.M., Brauer, M., Halverstadt, J. B., & Innes-Ker, A. H., (2001). When did her smile drop? Facial mimicry and the influences of emotional state on the detection of change in emotional expression. *Cognition and Emotion*, 15 (6), 853–864.

Niedenthal, P. M., Halberstadt, J. B., Margolin, J., & Innes-Ker, A. H. (2000). Emotional state and the detection of change in the facial expression of emotion. *European Journal of Social Psychology*, 30, 211–222.

Oberman, L. M., Pineda, J. A., & Ramachandran, V. S. (2007). The human mirror neuron system: a link between action observation and social skills. *Social, Cognitive, and Affective Neuroscience*, 2, 62–66.

Oberman, L. M., & Ramachandran, V. S. (2007). The simulating social mind: The role of the mirror neuron system and simulation in the social and communicative deficits of autism spectrum disorders. *Psychological Bulletin*, 133 (2), 310–327.

Ochsner, K. N., Bunge, S. A., Gross, J. J., & Gabrieli, J. D. E. (2002). Rethinking feelings: An fMRI study of the cognitive regulation of emotion. *Journal of Cognitive Neuroscience*, 14, 1215–1229.

O'Donohue, W., & Ferguson, K. E. (2001). *The psychology of B. F. Skinner*. Thousand Oaks, CA: Sage Publications.

Panksepp, J. (1998). *Affective neuroscience: The foundations of human and animal emotions*. New York: Oxford University Press.

Panksepp, J. (2008). The power of the word may reside in the power of affect. *Integrative Psychological and Behavioral Science*, 42(1), 47–55.

Pavuluri, M. N., O'Connor, M. M., Harral, E., & Sweeney, J. A. (2008). Affective neural circuitry during facial emotion processing in pediatric bipolar disorder. *Biological Psychiatry*, 162, 244–255.

Pecukonis, E. V. (1990). A cognitive/affective empathy training program as a function of ego development in aggressive adolescent females. *Adolescence*, 25, 59–76.

Pescosolido, A. T. (2005). Managing emotion: a new role for emergent group leaders, in C. Hartel, W. Zerbe, & N. Ashkanasy (Eds). *Emotions in Organizational Behaviors*, LAWRENCE-Erlbaum, London.

Pessoa, L., McKenna, M., Gutierrez, E., & Ungerleider, L. G. (2002). Neural processing of emotional faces requires attention. *Proceedings of the National Academy of Sciences USA*, 99, 11458–11463.

Pfeifer, J. H., Iacoboni, M., Mazziotta, J. C., & Dapretto, M. (2009). Mirroring others' emotions relates to empathy and interpersonal competence in children. *NeuroImage*, 39, 2076–2085.

Phelps, E. A., & LeDoux, J. E. (2005). Contributions of the amygdala to emotion processing: From animal models to human behavior. *Neuron*, 48, 175–187.

Porges, S. W. (1997). Emotion: An evolutionary by-product of the neural regulation of the autonomic nervous system. *Annals of the New York Academy of Sciences*, 807, 62–77.

Porges, S. W. (2004). Neuroception: A subconscious system for detecting threat and safety. *Zero to Three: Bulletin of the National Center for Clinical Infant Programs*, 24(5), 19–24.

Porges, S. W. (2009a). Reciprocal influences between body and brain in the perception and expression of affect: A polyvagal perspective. In D. Fosha, D. J. Siegel, & M. R. Salomon (Eds.), *The healing power of emotion: Affective neuroscience, development, clinical practice* (pp. 27–54). New York: Norton.

Posner, M. I., & Rothbart, M. K. (2007). *Educating the human brain.* Washington, DC: American Psychological Association.

Post, R. M., Weiss, S. R. B., Li, H., Smith, M. A., Zhang, L. X., Xing, G., et al. (1998). *Neural plasticity and emotional memory: Development and Psychopathology, 10,* 829–856.

Preston, S. D., & deWaal, F. B. (2002). Empathy: Its ultimate and proximate bases. *Behavioral and Brain Sciences, 25,* 1–72.

Price, J. L., Carmichael, S. T., & Drevets, W. C. (1996). Networks related to the orbital and medial prefrontal cortex: A substrate for emotional behavior? *Progress in Brain Research, 107,* 523–536.

Ramachandran, V. S. (2006, June 19). Mirror neurons and the brain in the vat. *Edge:The Third Culture.* Retrieved February 26, 2008, from the Edge:The Third Culture Web site: http://www.edge.org/3rd_culture/ramachandran06/ramachandran06_index.html.

Rankin, K. P., Gorno-Tempini, M. L., Allison, S. C., Stanley, C. M., Glenn, S., Weiner, M. W., & Miller, B. L. (2006). Structural anatomy of empathy in neurodegenerative disease. *Brain Sciences, 25,* 1–72.

Rath, T., & Chonchie, B. (2008). *Strength-based leadership, great leaders, teams and why people follow.* New York: Gallup Press.

Rauch, S. L., Shin, L. M., & Wright, C. I. (2003). Neuroimaging studies of amygdala function in anxiety disorders. *Annals of the New York Academy of Sciences, 985,* 389–410.

Redmond, M. (1985). The relationship between perceived communication competence and perceived empathy. *Communication Monographs, 52,* 377–382.

Restak, R. (2001). *The secret life of the brain.* Washington, DC: John Henry.

Richendoller, N. R., & Weaver, J. B., III (1994). Exploring the links between personality and empathic response style. *Personality and Individual Differences, 17,* 303–311.

Rizzolatti, G. (2005). The mirror neuron system and imitation. In S. Hurley & N. Chater (Eds.), *Perspectives on imitation: From neuroscience to social science: Vol. 1. Mechanisms of imitation and imitation in animals.* (pp. 55–76). Cambridge, MA: MIT Press.

Rizzolatti, G., & Craighero, L. (2004). The mirror-neuron system. *Annual Review of Neuroscience*, 27, 169–192.

Rizzolatti, G., Fadiga, L., Gallese, V., & Fogassi, L. (1996). Premotor cortex and the recognition of motor actions. *Cognitive Brain Research*, 3(2), 131–141.

Robinson, M. (2010). *Understanding behavior and development in early childhood: A guide to theory and practice.* New York: Routledge Publishing.

Rodrigues, S. M., LeDoux, J. E., Sapolsky, R. M. (2009). The influence of stress hormones on fear circuitry. *Annu Rev Neurosci* 32, 289–313.

Rogers, C. R. (1975). Empathic: An unappreciated way of being. *Counseling Psychologist*, 5, 2–10.

Rogers, C. R. (1980). The foundations of a person-centered approach. In C. Rogers (Ed.), *A way of being* (pp. 113–136). Boston, MA: Houghton-Mifflin.

Rolls, E. T. (1999). *The brain and emotion.* Oxford: Oxford University Press.

Ruby, P., & Decety, J. (2003). What you believe versus what you think they believe: A neuroimaging study of conceptual perspective-taking. *European Journal of Neuroscience*, 17, (11), 2475–2480.

Ruby, P., & Decety, J. (2004). How would you feel versus how do you think she would feel? A neuroimaging study of perspective taking with social emotions. *Journal of Cognitive Neuroscience*, 16(6): 988–999.

Ryan L., et al. (2001). Hippocampal complex and retrieval of recent and very remote autobiographical memories: evidence from functional magnetic resonance imaging in neurologically intact people. *Hippocampus* 11:707–14.

Saarela, M. V., Hluschchuk, Y., Williams, A. C., Schurmann, M., Dalso, E., & Hari, R. (2006). The compassionate brain: Humans detect intensity of pain from another's face. *Cerebral Cortex* 17, 230–237.

Salovey, P., & Gruel, D., (2005). The science of emotional intelligence. *Current Directions in Psychological Science*, 14, 281–285.

Salzberg, S., & Kabat-Zinn, J. (2008). *Lovingkindness: The revolutionary art of happiness.* Boston, MA: Shambhala.

Sanon-Fisher, R. W., & Poole, D.A. (1987). Training medical students to empathise: an experimental study. *Medical Journal of Australia*, 1, 473–6.

Sapolsky, R. M., Unio, H., Rebert, C. S., & Finch, C. E. (1990). Hippocampal damage associated with prolonged glucocorticoid exposure in primates. *J Neurosci* 10:2897–902.

Saxe, R., & Kanwisher, N. (2003). People thinking about thinking people. The role of the temporo-parietal junction in "theory of mind." *NeuroImage*, 19(4), 1835–1842.

Saxe, R., & Wexler, A. (2005). Making sense of another mind: The role of the right temporo-parietal junction. *Neuropsychologia*, 43(10), 1391–1399.

Schaller, M., & Cialdini, R. D. (1988). The economics of empathic helping: Support for a mood management motive. *Journal of Experimental Social Psychology*, 24, 163–181.

Scherer, K. R., Schorr, A., & Johnstone, T. (2001). *Appraisal processes in emotion*. New York: Oxford University Press.

Schore, A. N. (1994). *Affect regulation and the origin of the self: The neurobiology of emotional development*. New York: Erlbaum.

Schore, A. N. (2003). *Affect regulation and the repair of the self*. New York: Norton.

Schore, A. N. (2003, March). New developments in attachment theory: Application to clinical practice, Lifespan Learning Institute UCLA, Attachment Conference, Los Angeles, CA.

Schore, A. N. (2005). A neuropsychoanalytic viewpoint: Commentary on paper by Steven H. Knoblauch. *Psychoanalytic Dialogues*, 15, 829–854.

Schore, A. N. (2005). Back to basics: Attachment, affect regulation, and the right brain: Linking developmental neuroscience to pediatrics. *Pediatrics in Review* 26(6), 204–217.

Schulte-Rüther, M., Markowitsch, H. J., Fink, G. R., & Piefke, M. (2007). Mirror neuron and theory of mind mechanisms involved in face-to-face interactions: A functional magnetic resonance imaging approach to empathy. *Journal of Cognitive Neuroscience*, 19, 54–72.

Schwartz, J. M., & Begley, S. (2002). *The mind and the brain: Neuroplasticity and the power of mental force*. New York: Harper Collins.

Selby, John (2007). *Listening with empathy, creating genuine connections with customers and colleagues*. Charlottesville, VA: Hampton Roads Publishing Co.

Seligman, M. (1991). *Learned Optimism*. New York: Knopf.

Shamay-Tsoory, S. G., Tomer, R., Berger, B. D., & Aharon-Peretz, J. (2003). Characterization of empathy deficits following prefrontal brain damage: The role of the right ventromedial prefrontal cortex. *Journal of Cognitive Neuroscience*, 15, 324–337.

Shamay-Tsoory, S. G., Tomer, R., Goldsher, D., Berger, B. D., & Aharon-Peretz, J. (2004). Impairment in cognitive and affective empathy in patients with brain lesions: Anatomical and cognitive correlates. *Journal of Clinical and Experimental Neuropsychology*, 26, 1113–1127.

Shapiro, J. (2002). How do physicians teach empathy in the primary care setting? *Academic Medicine*, 77, 323–328.

Siegel, D. J. (1996). Cognitive neuroscience encounters psychotherapy: Lessons from research on attachment and the development of emotion, memory and narrative. *Psychiatric Times*, 13(3), 143–148.

Siegel, D. J. (1999). *The developing mind: How relationship and the brain interact to shape who we are.* New York: Guilford Press.

Siegel, D. J. (2006). An interpersonal neurobiology approach to psychotherapy: Awareness, mirror neurons, and neural plasticity in the development of well being. *Psychiatric Annals*, 36(4), 247–258.

Siegel, D. J. (2007). *The mindful brain: Reflection and attunement in the cultivation of well-being.* New York: Norton.

Siegel, D. J. (2007). Mindfulness training and neural integration: Differentiation of distinct streams of awareness and the cultivation of well-being. *Social, Cognitive, and Affective Neuroscience*, 2, 259–263.

Siegel, D. J. (2010a). *Mindsight: The new science of personal transformation.* New York: Bantam.

Simon, D., Craig, K. D., Miltner, W. H. R., & Rainville, P. (2006). Brain responses to dynamic facial expressions of pain. *Pain*, 126, 309–318.

Singer, T. (2006). The neuronal basis and ontogeny of empathy and mind reading: Review of literature and implications for future research. *Neuroscience and Biobehavioral Reviews*, 30(6), 855-863. Doi:10.1016/j.neubiorev.2006.06.011.

Singer, T., & Frith, C. (2005). The painful side of empathy: Comment. *Nature neuroscience*, 8, 845–846.

Singer, T., Seymour, B., O'Doherty, J., Kaube H., Dolan, R.J., & Frith, C.D. (2004). Empathy for pain involves the affective but not sensory components of pain. *Science*, 303, 1157–1162.

Skinner, B. F. (1938). 'Superstition' in the pigeon. *Journal of Experimental Psychology*, 38, pp. 168–172.

Small, D., and J. S. Lerner. (2006). "Emotional policy: Personal sadness and anger shape policy judgements." *Political Psychology* (Special Issue on Emotion in Politics).

Sommerville, J. A., & Decety, J. (2006). Weaving the fabric of social interaction: Articulating developmental psychology and cognitive neuroscience in the domain of motor cognition. *Psychonomic Bulletin and Review*, 13(2), 179–200.

Spinella, M. (2005). Prefrontal substrates of empathy: Psychometric evidence in a community sample. *Biological Psychology*, 70, 175–181.

Squire, L. R. (1998). Memory system. *CR Acad Sci* III 321:153–6.

Squire, L. R., Knowlton, B., Musen, G. (1993). The structure and organization of memory. *Annu Rev Psychol* 44, 453–95.

Stein, M. B., Goldin, P. R., Sareen, J., Zorrila, L. T., & Brown, G. G. (2002). Increased amygdala activation to angry and contemptuous faces in generalized social phobia. *Archives of General Psychiatry*, 59, 1027–1034.

Stephan, W. G., & Finley, K. (1999). The role of empathy in improving intergroup relations. *Journal of Social Issues*, 55, 729–743.

Stiff, J. B, Dillard, J. P., Somera, L., Kim, H., & Sleight, C. (1988). Empathy, communication and prosocial behavior. *Communication Monographs*, 55, 198–213.

Stone, V. E. (2006). Theory of mind and the evolution of social intelligence. In J. T. Cacioppo, P. S. Visser, & C. L. Pickett (Eds.), *Social neuroscience: People thinking about thinking people* (pp. 103–129). Cambridge, MA: MIT Press.

Stout, C. (1999). The art of empathy: Teaching students to care. *Art Education*, 52, 21–24, 33–34.

Stuss, D. T., Gallup, G. G., & Alexander, M. P. (2001). The frontal lobes are necessary for "theory of mind." *Brain*, 124, 279–286.

Sunderland, M. (2006). *The science of parenting: How today's brain research can help you raise happy, emotionally balanced children*. New York: DK Publishing.

Suslow, T., et al. (2006). Amygdala activation during masked presentation of emotional faces predicts conscious detection of threat-related faces. *Brain Cogn* 61:243–8.

Tag archives: empathy. Lead Change Group (April 8, 2013). Available at http://leadchangegroup.com/tag/empathy/ and http://leadchangegroup.com/5-leadership-approaches-for-knowing-being-and-doing/.

Taylor, F. W. (1911). *The principles of scientific management.* New York: Harper & Row.

The Role of Empathy in Business Success. SmartBlog (April 8, 2013). Available at http://smartblogs.com/leadership/2013/04/01/the-role-of-empathy-in-business-success/.

Thomas, K. (2009). *Intrinsic motivation at work: What really drives employee engagement* (Second Edition). San Francisco, CA: Berrett-Koehler Publishers.

Titchener, E. (1909). *Elementary psychology of the thought processes.* New York: Macmillan.

Tomkins, S. (1987). Shame. In P. Ekman (Ed.), *Emotion in the human face* (p. 137). New York: Guildford Press.

Trevarthen, C. (2001). Intrinsic motives for companionship in understanding: Their origin, development, and significance for infant mental health. *Infant Mental Health Journal,* 22, pp. 95–131.

Trout, J.D. (2009). *Why empathy matters, The judgment and psychology of better judgment.* New York: The Penguin Group.

Urry, H. L., Nitschke, J. B., Dolski, I., Jackson, D. C., Dalton, K. M., Mueller, C. J., et al. (2004). Making a life worth living: Neural correlates of well-being. *Psychological Science,* 15(6), 367–372.

Vaadia, E., et al. (1995). Dynamics of neuronal interaction in the monkey cortex in relation to behavioral events. *Nature,* 373, 515–18.

Vanaerscot, G. (1990). The process of empathy: Holding and letting go. In G. Lietaer, J. Rombauts, & R. Van Balen (Eds.). *Client-centered and experiential psychotherapy in the nineties* (pp. 269–294). Leuven, Belgium: Leuven University Press.

Van Baaren, R. B., Holland, R. W., Kawakami, K., & van Knippenberg, A. (2004). Mimicry and prosocial behavior. *Psychological Science,* 15 (1), 71–74.

Van Stegeren, A. H., et al. (1998). Memory for emotional events: Differential effects of centrally versus peripherally acting beta blocking agents. *Psychopharmacology* (Berl) 138, 305–10.

Vollm, B. A., Taylor, A. N., Richardson, P., Corcoran, R., Stirling, J., McKie, S., Deakin, J. F., & Elliott, R. (2006). Neuronal correlates of theory of mind and empathy: A functional magnetic resonance imaging study in a nonverbal task. *NeuroImage, 29*, 90–98.

Vroom, V. H. (1964). *Work and Motivation*. New York, NY: Wiley.

Vuilleumier, P. (2005). How brains beware; neural mechanisms of emotional attention. *Trends Cogn Sci 9*, 585–94.

Vuilleumier, P., Armony, J. L., Driver, J., & Dolan, R. J. (2001). Effects of attention and emotion on face processing in the human brain: An event-related fMRI study. *Neuron, 30* (3), 829–841.

Vuilleumier, P., Armony, J. L., Driver, J., & Dolan, R. J. (2003). Distinct spatial frequency sensitivities for processing faces and emotional expressions. *Nature Neuroscience, 6*(6), 624–631.

Wallace, B. A. (2006). *The attention revolution: Unlocking the power of the focused mind*. Somerville, MA: Wisdom Publications.

Warner, M. S., (1997). Does empathy cure? A theoretical consideration of empathy, processing, and personal narrative. In A. C. Bohart & L. S. Greenberg (Eds.). *Empathy reconsidered: New directions in psychotherapy* (pp. 125–140). Washington, DC: American Psychological Association.

Watson, J. C. (2001). Revisioning empathy: Theory, research and practice. In D. Cain & J. Seeman (Eds.), *Handbook of research and practice in humanistic psychotherapy* (pp. 445–472). New York: American Psychological Association.

Watson, J. C., Goldman, R., & Vanaerschot, G. (1998). Empathic: A postmodern way of being. In L. S. Greenberg, J. C. Watson, & G. Lietaer (Eds.), *Handbook of experiential psychotherapy.* (pp. 61–81). New York: Guilford Press.

Weaver, J. B., & Kirtley, M. D. (1994). Listening styles and empathy. *Southern Communication Journal, 59*, 131–140.

What is Empathy? *Skills You Need* (April 8, 2013). Available at www.skillsyouneed.com/ips/empathy.html.

What's Empathy Got to Do with It? *Mindtools* (April 8, 2013). Available at http://www.mindtools.com/pages/article/newLDR_75.htm.

Wicker, B., Keysers, C., Plailly, J., Royet, J. P., Gallese, V., & Rizzolatti, G. (2003). Both of us disgusted in my insula: The common neural basis of seeing and feeling disgust. *Neuron, 40*(3), 655–664.

Wild, B., Erv, M., & Bartels, M. (2001). Are emotions contagious? Evoked emotions while viewing emotionally expressive faces: Quality, quantity, time course and gender differences. *Psychiatry Research*, 102, 109–124.

Wild, B., Erb, M., Eyb M., Bartels, M., & Grodd, W. (2003). Why are smiles contagious? An fMRI study of the interaction between perception of facial affect and facial movements. *Psychiatry Research: Neuroimaging*, 123, 17–36.

Wilson, M., & Knoblich, G. (2005). The case for motor involvement in perceiving conspecifics. *Psychological Bulletin*, 131, 460–473.

Winkielman, P., Zajonc, R.B., and Schwarz, N. (1997). "Subliminal Affective Priming Resists Attributional Interventions." *Cognition and Emotion*, 11, 433–465.

Winston, J. S., O'Doherty, J., & Dolan, R. J. (2003). Common and distinct neural responses during direct and incidental processing of multiple facial emotions. *NeuroImage*, 20 (1) 84–97.

Winston, J. S., Strange, B. A., O'Doherty, J., & Dolan, R. J. (2002). Automatic and intentional brain responses during evaluation of trustworthiness of faces. *Nature Neuroscience*, 5, 277–283.

Wynn, R., & Wynn, M. (2006). Empathy as an interactionally achieved phenomenon in psychotherapy. *Journal of Pragmatics*, 38, 1385–1397.

Zahn-Waxler, C., Radke-Yarrow, M., Wagner, E., & Chapman, M. (1992). Development of empathic concern for others. *Developmental Psychology*, 28, 126–136.

Zajonc, R.B. (1980). Feeling and thinking: Preferences need no inferences. *American Psychologist*, 35, 151–175.

Zeidner, M., Roberts, R. D., & Mathews, G. (2002). Can emotional intelligence be schooled? A critical review. *Educational Psychologist*, 37(4), 215–231.

Zillman, D. (1991). Empathy: Affect from bearing witness to the emotions of others. In J. Bryant & D. Zillman (Eds.), *Responding to the screen: Reception and reaction processes* (pp. 135–167). Hillsdale, NJ: Erlbaum.

CPSIA information can be obtained at www.ICGtesting.com
Printed in the USA
LVOW13s2247270614

392152LV00003B/4/P